# Cost Shifting and the Freezing of Corporate Pension Plans

Since the early 1980s, there has been a shift from defined benefit (DB) to defined contribution (DC) pension arrangements in the U.S. corporate sector. This shift has continued markedly over the past decade. In the late 1990s, assets in private sector DB and DC plans were each around $2 trillion. By the end of 2010, DB plan assets in the private sector amounted to $2.5 trillion, compared to $3.8 trillion of DC assets.[1]

The shift towards DC plans has occurred through several channels. First, the majority of new firms have favored DC arrangements. Second, some private sector sponsors of DB pension plans have entered bankruptcy and terminated their plans, transferring unfunded liabilities to the Pension Benefit Guarantee Corporation (PBGC). Finally, many firms have limited or stopped new DB accruals by implementing a partial or complete freeze of these accruals. Firms undertaking a "soft freeze" have allowed DB benefits to continue to accrue for existing workers while offering new workers a DC plan only. Firms undertaking a "hard freeze" have stopped DB accruals entirely for all workers.

While workers do not lose defined benefits that they have earned up to the date of a hard freeze, their defined benefit pension ceases to grow with future work or pay increases. In place of the DB accruals, the employer offers a DC plan, making contributions that are specified as a share of payroll or that match employee contributions up to a limit. By 2011, 40% of DB pension plan sponsors in the *Fortune* 1000 had at least one frozen plan.[2]

In a competitive, frictionless labor market, the freezing of pension benefits would not result in any cost saving for firms or reduction in total compensation for workers. Workers would simply receive contributions to DC plans that offset the loss of DB accruals, or alternatively they would demand and receive offsetting wage increases. In contrast, if under pre-freeze pay and benefit arrangements some workers are receiving compensation in excess of their marginal product (or would under the DB arrangement receive such excess compensation in the future), the firm could potentially realize cost savings through a freeze. If workers value DB benefits less than it costs the firm to provide them, there would be a surplus over which employers and employees could bargain and both parties could be made better off with a freeze.

---

[1] See Department of Labor (2011), http://www.dol.gov/ebsa/pdf/historicaltables.pdf .
[2] See Towers Watson (2011).

Starting from a comprehensive sample of DB plans in the U.S., this paper studies the prospective accrual patterns of firms that freeze pension plans versus those that do not, in order to shed light on two questions.

First, how much annual cost saving is realized by firms that freeze, taking into account both the DB accruals that they avoid and the increases in DC contributions that they make? Net of the increase in total DC contributions, firms are estimated to save around 2.7-3.6% of payroll per year. Workers would have to value the structure, choice, flexibility, or portability of DC plans by at least this much more to experience welfare gains from freezes, as we find no evidence of compensating salary increases. From the perspective of the firm freezing the plan, the savings amount to around 0.4% of total book assets per year.

Second, do firms that freeze their DB plans ("freeze firms") have larger potential cost savings in the form of counterfactual DB accruals than comparable firms that do not? We find that freeze firms would face higher expected DB accruals as a share of firm assets in the absence of a freeze than comparable firms that do not freeze, and that the probability that a firm freezes a pension plan is positively related to the value of new accruals as a share of firm assets. We then decompose the accrual differences for freeze and non-freeze firms into benefit-related parameters, demographic factors, and the size of the labor force relative to firm assets. While freeze firms have more workers in the 55-64 age range than firms that do not, they have fewer workers in the 35-54 age range. We find that much of the difference in prospective accruals between the freeze and matched non-freeze firms is driven by the size of the labor force relative to firm assets, as well as differences in benefit factors.

The DB accrual estimates emerge from a simple model with parameters calibrated to the accruals that firms report in administrative filings on the IRS 5500 form. This allows us to capture heterogeneity in the generosity of benefits across plans. Having obtained both density and salary distributions by age and service from the appendices to the forms, we can build the accruals by plan for each specific age and salary group. The approach also allows for a decomposition of the results by age and service. Assuming that the employer's DC plan contributions as a share of salary are constant across age groups, realized cost savings by firms is largest for workers aged 50-65 and smallest for workers aged 20-34. The forgone accruals and net cost effects are initially largest for older employees but over time become largest for middle-aged employees who plan to stay with the firms until retirement.

These measurements have several broad implications for economic theory. The ability of employers to achieve cost savings of these magnitudes by changing pension arrangements without providing other compensating differentials to employees is consistent with the hypothesis that strong labor market frictions are prevalent among DB sponsors. That is, either the employees of these firms had been earning more than their marginal product before the freeze, or after the freeze they are earning less. The freeze represents a significant and sudden change to compensation that cannot plausibly be a reflection of one-year changes in the worker's marginal product. One plausible explanation is that substantial frictions or adjustment costs exist for DB sponsors that limit the extent to which compensation can be adjusted to equal marginal cost on an annual basis. An alternative hypothesis is that workers simply do not value DB pension benefits. This would be consistent with literature suggesting that individuals undervalue annuities but less consistent with the economic theory that suggests such benefits provide valuable longevity insurance.

This paper proceeds as follows. Section 1 discusses the institutional background, existing literature, and theoretical considerations. Section 2 considers data and methodology. In Section 3 we present the results. Section 4 concludes.

## 1. Background, Literature, and Theoretical Considerations
### 1.1. Institutional background

DB plans were the predominant vehicle for retirement two decades ago. Encouraged by the tax deductibility of pension contributions in times when corporate tax rates reached historical highs, these plans were viewed as a tool to build and retain human capital. Their importance has steadily declined in the US with the introduction of DC plans, particularly 401(k) plans, in the early 1980s. There are many differences between DB and DC plans but perhaps the single most important is the distribution of risk between employer and employee.

DB plan sponsors promise fixed retirement income to their employees, with employers bearing all the investment risk to meet the pension liability. The risk borne by the employee under a DB plan is limited to risk of job change, risk that future benefit accruals will be reduced or eliminated (as in a freeze), salary risk (since the pension is a function of late-career salary), and risk that the accrued benefits will be reduced if their employer becomes financially insolvent. The employer bears investment risk and longevity risk. DC plans typically give most or all responsibility to the employee for making their own contributions, bearing investment risk, and making financial decisions. The sponsor responsibility in a DC plan arrangement essentially ends after its share of the contribution is made.

The decline of DB pensions has been documented beginning with early work by Clark and McDermed (1990) and Gustman and Steinmeier (1992). According to figures by Buessing and Soto (2006), the number of individuals with only a DB plan fell from 9.6 million in 1990 to 6.6 million in 2003, whereas the number of individuals with only a DC plan rose from 11.5 million to 30.1 million over the same time period.

One heavily cited reason behind the shift is the significant increase in pension costs and risks to the employer. The employer bears the risk of DB plan investments. It also bears interest rate risk, which affects the present value of the pension liability and therefore the mandatory funding requirements. Life expectancy rates today are longer than they were 20-30 years ago when the plans were adopted. DB plans imposed large costs on many employers during the first half of this decade, as poor asset market returns combined with low interest rates led to large cash funding requirements. In many instances, the pension plan becomes a competing interest for cash within the organization.

Changing legislation has also altered expectations about costs. The Pension Protection Act (PPA) of 2006 tightened funding requirements for most industries and new accounting standards (FASB 158) have moved some liabilities onto the balance sheet that were previously off the balance sheet. Another possible reason for the shift is the desire to align employee compensation with the lower labor cost of global competitors. In equilibrium, the sum of cash wages and fringe benefits declines with competition, and employers find it easier to cut pension benefits.

Facing all these challenges, corporate DB sponsors may prefer the less costly and more manageable structure of DC plans, other things equal. However, the termination of a DB plan is often costly and in many cases not possible. Unfunded pension liabilities can be taken over by PBGC only when the sponsor has filed for bankruptcy. Under normal business conditions, plans can only be terminated if they are fully funded. In this case, a 50% excise tax is applied to any excess assets reverted to the employer, followed by another layer of corporate income taxes. However, if participants in a terminating plan are provided with a replacement plan, the excise tax is reduced to 20%.[3] If they decide to proceed, sponsors must pay off beneficiaries by purchasing annuities. Most of these "standard terminations" have been implemented for small single employer plans.[4] The number of "distress terminations" is also small, but the large ones have been highly publicized (for example United Airlines).

The most common strategy for putting an end to new accruals is a pension freeze. By freezing DB plans and increasing employee participation in DC plans, firms relax the mandatory nature of future benefit payments give themselves greater future flexibility, and reduce their operating leverage (Petersen (1994)).

While there are several types of freezes, all involve the reduction or the cessation of new accruals. A hard freeze eliminates all future accruals, so that the benefits will not grow from the level they reached at the time of the freeze. A soft freeze typically eliminates new accruals based on years of service, in particular by closing the plan to new employees. Most often, sponsoring companies compensate workers by allowing them to participate in either an existing or a new 401(k) plan.[5] Many large companies sponsor more than one plan, and firms frequently decide to freeze plans on a selective basis.

As an alternative or predecessor to freezing, some companies have undertaken conversions of their existing DB plans to hybrid plans called cash balance (CB) plans. In this arrangement, the employer contributions are pooled and invested by the sponsor, who promises a minimum guaranteed rate of return (Clark and Schieber (2004), Coronado and Copeland (2004)). In order to protect accrued benefits, the starting cash balance is typically based on the present value of the cash flows the worker would have received under the DB arrangement. The account is then credited every year with a 'pay credit' (a fixed percentage of salary) and an 'interest

---

[3] For this to take effect, the employer must demonstrate that he amended the plan prior to termination to provide immediate pro-rate benefit increases and that he transferred 25% of the terminating plan's excess assets directly to the replacement plan before any amount was reverted.

[4] According to Belt (2005), during the 1986-1994 period, 99,000 of the 101,000 single-employer plan terminations fell into the category of a standard termination, with only 2,000 being distress terminations.

[5] The PBGC has calculated that as of 2003, 9.4% of DB plans were frozen (PBGC (2005)), and other studies have calculated that the occurrence of plans being frozen to new participants is even more prevalent than the PBGC suggests (VanDerhei (2006)).

credit' (fixed rate or a rate tied to T-bill rate). The present value of the balance grows more linearly, replacing the more convex increase in pension value that would have occurred under the DB plan.[6] As in the traditional DB plans, benefits do not depend on the plan's investment performance. Having replaced DB accruals with the generally smaller CB accruals, the sponsor still has the option to freeze the CB accruals at a later date. If the sponsor freezes the CB plan, the CB accruals are then replaced with contributions to a DC plan.

## 1.2. Related Literature

Previous literature on the role of DB plans in the corporation have focused on work incentives (Ippolito (1985), Lazear (1983)), tax benefits (Black (1980), Tepper (1981), Petersen (1992), Shivdasani and Stefanescu (2010)), earnings manipulation (Bergstresser, Desai, and Rauh (2006)) and financial slack (Ballester, Fried and Livnat (2002)). Corporate pension plans have a significant impact on the investment policy of the company (Rauh (2006)) and in some pension systems, significant agency conflicts can exist between the insider trustees and plan members (Cocco and Volpin (2007)).

A substantial literature also examines the differential risk characteristics of DB and DC plans. Bodie, Marcus, and Merton (1988) model the basic tradeoffs as relating to which party (employer or employee) bears the risks of asset returns, inflation, longevity, and salaries. Samwick and Skinner (2004) and Poterba et al (2007) evaluate DB versus DC wealth accumulation through simulations with either synthetic or actual earnings histories, with the finding that based on historical distributions, DC plans provide employees with higher average mean benefits but a greater likelihood of very low wealth outcomes. The findings in these papers reflect to some extent the relatively high equity risk premium implied by historical data, to which participants in DC plans have direct exposure.

Comparisons of DB pension wealth and DC pension wealth are complicated by the fact that while accrued DC pension wealth can be observed directly, accrued DB pension wealth is the present value of a future stream of promised benefit payments. An earlier literature examined how DB pension accruals affect labor market behavior (e.g. Lazear (1983), Mitchell and Fields

---

[6] Most cash balance plans have an annuitization option. Conversely, many traditional DB plans also allow participants to take benefits as lump sums. The key difference between a traditional DB plan and a cash balance plan is therefore the accrual pattern, not the form of the benefit.

(1984)). However, more recently the literature also suggest a shift on the supply side, as labor characteristics and preferences have changed (e.g. Aaronson and Coronado (2005)). As emphasized by Lazear and Moore (1988) and Stock and Wise (1990), the option to continue to earn benefits under a DB plan is valuable in addition to the accrued defined benefits, particularly if vesting periods are long, and as such the labor market decisions of pension plan participants should also be a function of this option value. If firms can freeze DB plans at their option, however, then the option value component of future DB plan participation for participants is at least in part diminished. In this paper we use the flow of DB accruals as the measure of the compensation cost of DB pensions to the firm, under the implicit assumption that firms have the option to freeze DB accruals.

The literature has succeeded in modeling some of the potential macroeconomic forces behind the DB to DC shift, such as declines in the value of existing jobs relative to new jobs (Friedberg and Owyang (2004)) and reduced search costs (Friedberg et al (2006)). Studies by Kruse (1995) and Ippolito and Thompson (2000) examine the periods 1980-1986 and 1987-2005 and find that the growth in DC plans over those periods was more the result of compositional effects than of terminating DB plans or of DC conversions. However, these studies came before the hybrid conversions and pension freezes of very large employers. Pension freezes became common in the early 2000s. In 2005, for example, IBM, Hewlett Packard, Sears Holding, Verizon and many other firms announced pension freezes. Reports issued by the Pension Benefit Corporation (2008), Government Accountability Office (2008) and Towers Watson (2012) show that the majority of the freezes affect small plans. They show that about 21 percent of all currently active DB participants have been affected by a freeze and that almost half of all sponsors have at least one frozen plan.

Given the relatively recent wave of freezes (and the lag with which this information becomes available at the plan level), the determinants of the decision to freeze DB plan have not been completely understood. To our knowledge, Munnell and Soto (2007) is the only paper that carries out an analysis that combines both the sponsor and the plan level characteristics, exploring cross-sectional differences in 2005. They find the plan characteristics (underfunding level, size, large credit balances, bargaining power) play a role in the firm decision to freeze, and the financial health of the company has a small economic impact on the decision to freeze. In contrast, Beaudoin and al. (2010) find that the profitability of the sponsor is important. In addition, they show that the balance sheet impact of SFAS 158 is associated with the decision to freeze.

The set of potential explanatory factors for pension freezes is thus rather large. A non-exhaustive list would include: a firm's incentive to reduce employee compensation costs, the firm's desire to reduce volatility of cash flows, the demand of employees for more portable benefits, the relative effects of the two types of plans on reported accounting income, whether the firm is a federal contractor receiving reimbursed contributions (Morgensen (2011)), industrial competitiveness, and the impact of financial flexibility on operating leverage (Petersen (1994)).

We focus in this paper on estimating the potential and realized cost savings at the plan level, in absolute value and also relative to a sample of control plans. To the extent that we find positive cost savings in present value, it can be said that employees would need to value the structural features of DC plans by at least that much in order to be indifferent as a result of the switch. We also examine whether accrual costs matter to firms in making the decision to freeze plans, and specifically whether those firms facing higher accruals are more likely to freeze, controlling for other firm and plan characteristics.

Several papers have attempted to use equity market event studies to examine a closely related question, specifically whether DB plan freezes enhance shareholder value. Positive stock market announcement returns would indicate that the market believes that the cost reductions due to freezes will not be offset by other cost increases, in other words that freezes enhance shareholder value. However, due perhaps to the challenges of identifying the exact moment in time when the information about pension freezes was impounded by markets, this literature has been somewhat inconclusive. Rubin (2007) finds that pension freezes enhance firm market values with a lag, which would be consistent with long-run cost savings if markets focus on the short-run flows and do not capitalize long-run cost savings until they are evident in cash flows. Milevsky and Song (2008) find a positive impact of DB freezing on company value of around 3.8% but of marginal statistical significance. McFarland, Pang, and Warshawsky (2009) find in fact small firm value declines in some specifications. They argue that 401(k) enhancements and declines in employee productivity may offset any potential cost savings, or alternatively that freezes are simply a reflection of financial challenges at the firm. In the sense that our paper considers the cost effects on the firm from a cash flow and accrual standpoint, it is complementary to this strand of literature.

### 1.3. Theoretical Considerations

In competitive and frictionless labor market equilibrium, a worker's total annual compensation must equal his or her annual marginal product of labor. Economic theory has posited a number of reasons why compensation may deviate from a worker's outside option. For example, efficiency wages may be paid to encourage effort (Shapiro and Stiglitz (1984)). Implicit contracts in which workers are paid less than their marginal product at the beginning of their career, and more than their marginal product late in the career, may discourage worker shirking (Lazear (1979)).

Under typical DB pension benefit rules, accruals are larger for older workers than for younger workers. This arrangement may arise because a firm's older workers are more productive than younger workers, or it may be that the firm is using the implicit contract of the pension plan to reduce turnover or agency problems.

A freeze of DB pension accruals can be thought of as having three sets of effects. First, the freeze in isolation with no offsets would be a cut in employee compensation; this cut is larger for longer-tenured employees whose annual accruals are larger. Hence, when considered in isolation, freezes lower DB pension accruals to zero and reduce the extent of seniority compensation.

Second, the firm may need to compensate employees affected by the freeze. The firm may do this by raising salaries or contributions to other benefit plans, including DC pension arrangements. In a perfectly competitive labor market in which employees and employers valued the pension benefits identically, the change in non-pension compensation should exactly offset the reduction in pension benefit accruals. All potential cost savings for the firm would be offset, and relative total compensation among young and old workers would be the same as they had been before the freeze. In contrast, these offsets will be small if workers were compensated more than their marginal products before the freeze. Alternatively, if workers had valued the pension benefits at an amount less than the cost to the employer of providing those benefits, freezing the pension plan would generate a surplus over which employers and employees could bargain.

Third, workers themselves may respond to the changed compensation package by pursuing outside options. If the total compensation of some workers relative to their outside options has decreased, then turnover for those workers would be expected to increase.

Given these effects, there are several sets of conditions that would induce a firm to freeze DB plans. For example, a firm whose longer-service workers were being compensated more than their marginal product under the DB plan in the context of some type of wage rigidities might attempt to freeze the plans to improve their competitive position. Firms that are in a weak financial position might also be induced to freeze plans in order to save costs, but only if actual cost savings could be achieved through the freeze. Freezing is likely to be more costly for firms facing stronger employee representation in the form of unions.

## 2. Data and Methodology
### 2.1. Data

Our primary source of information is Form 5500 filed annually by plan administrators with the Department of Labor (DOL) and the Internal Revenue Service (IRS). The information is compiled electronically by the DOL and made available on their website. We begin by extracting information on all DB plans filing the form between 1999 and 2010.[7] Next, we restrict the sample to the subset of plans that can be reliably linked to sponsors covered by Compustat.

The reported sponsor name and its employer identification number (EIN) serve as the primary identifiers. While these variables allow us to generate a first link to Compustat sponsors, in many instances the Form 5500 reports the name and the EIN of one of the parent sponsor's subsidiaries. Under the current IRS rules, subsidiaries that are at least 80% owned by the parent may elect to file consolidated income tax returns. But they can also choose to file taxes separately while still remaining consolidated with the parent company for financial purposes. In this case, the EIN and the sponsor name reported in Form 5500 will differ from its parent's. To overcome these problems we manually collect the names of all subsidiaries reported by all sponsors in the 10-k filings (Exhibit 21). We identify potential sponsors in Compustat based on the availability of aggregate pension information such as pension assets and liabilities. This process allows us to obtain a very close match between sponsors and plans. We describe our

---

[7] We work with the September 2011 update of the dataset. DOL compiles and posts the most recent filings on a monthly basis. These updates include amendments of filings from previous years as well as late filings.

sample selection in Table I. In the end, we are able to reliably match 40,637 plan-years to Compustat.

The sample is further restricted by the availability of age-service tables at the plan level. Under the current disclosure rules only plans with more than 1,000 active participants are required to disclose this information. We therefore restrict the sample to plans that report 1,000 active participants for at least one year during our sample period. This limits the sample to 14,315 plan-year observations. The age-service tables are reported in the paper attachments to Form 5500, they are not in a standardized form or collected electronically.[8] An example of this table is reported in the Appendix. Adding a small subgroup of matrices from earlier years that were obtainable from DOL, we are able to identify age-service tables for 8,551 plan-years.[9]

Most of the tables include both the number of participants and the average salary per participant, within each age-service group. However, for confidentiality reasons the salary information is only disclosed for age-service groups with more than 20 participants. We therefore estimate the average salary in these age-service groups (where the number of participants is available) by using information on disclosed salaries for the other age-service groups for that plan year and in the plan time series. The imputation relies on the following estimation, using the time series information on all available plans, at the age-service group level:

$$Log(Salary_{wpt}) = \alpha_1 + \alpha_2 Age_{wt} + \alpha_3 Age_{wt}^2 + \alpha_4 Service_{wt} + \alpha_5 Service_{wt}^2 + \varepsilon_p + \vartheta_t + \delta_{wpt}$$

where $Salary_{wp}$ is the average salary for participant $w$ in plan $p$, $Age$ and $Service$ are the age and the service groups for participant $w$, $\varepsilon_p$ is the plan fixed effect, $\vartheta_t$ is the time fixed effect and $\delta_{wpt}$ is the residual term. We run the regressions separately for cash balance (CB) plans and for traditional DB plans, allowing the possibility that the salaries of participants in CB plans follow a different path. There are 2,049 plan-years forms that are filed by cash balance plans. Where

---

[8] The Department of Labor made publicly available Form 5500 attachments during the summer of 2011, for all years between 2003- 2011. We hired a data service to manually enter the data from these age-service matrices into excel spreadsheets, and we subsequently standardized them for a uniform definition of age and service groups.
[9] The results are not sensitive to the inclusion or exclusion of the roughly 100 observations obtainable for 1999-2002. We requested this subset of paper attachments based on a pilot of sample plan freezes that we identified from public news announcements.

available, we also collect the cash balance table which reports individual account balances by age-service groups.

Next, we identify all plan-years where administrators report that a hard-freeze is in effect (897 plan-years). Once the plan is reported as frozen, all subsequent filings should have this annotation. This disclosure has been implemented in Form 5500 from 2003, although a few early adopters (or maybe late filers) have reported them for earlier years as well.

Identifying the year when the plan has been first frozen is very important for our analysis. We find that many of these plans report the freeze in Form 5500 with a long delay. In other cases the plans have been frozen years before they were required to report it. We search for information about plan freezes in the news, annual reports and in the history of the plan as reported in the attachments to Form 5500. We eliminate freezes implemented before our sample period and freezes associated with plan spin-offs or restructuring in the years preceding the freeze. We tabulate the year distributions of the sample pension freezes in Table II. Our procedure identifies 213 plans that have been frozen during our sample period. Of these, only 175 report the age-service table before the freeze is actually implemented. 52 of the 175 plans have a cash balance feature prior to the announcement.

## 2.2. Calibration of Benefit Parameters

DB plan features can be complex. In estimating benefit accruals for the traditional DB plans, we make a simplifying assumption that plan benefits take the form of years worked ($N_t$) times final salary ($Y_t$) times a benefit factor ($k$).[10] Measuring the change in benefit accruals over any given horizon therefore requires two plan level parameters: the benefit factor (or the percent benefit accrual) per year and the rate of salary growth.

*a. The benefit factor* ($k$). We estimate the benefit factor by using past information on expected service cost from Form 5500, at the plan level. More specifically, we calculate the service cost for each participant in each age-service group (or cell) and then we aggregate this information at the plan level.

---

[10] Final pay is most commonly used in the benefit formula. In practice, there are instances where employers take into account the career average pay or integrate the formula with Social Security benefits.

$$SC_{wt} = kZ_{t+1}N_{t+1}Y_{t+1} - kZ_tN_tY_t = kZ_t[(N_t+1)(1+i)Y_{t+1} - N_tY_t]$$

where $SC_{wt}$ is the service cost for participant w in year t, k is the plan level benefit factor, $N_t$ is the number of years the employee has worked as of time t, $Y_t$ is the employee's salary as of time t and i is the plan level discount rate (as reported in Form 5500). $Z_t$ is a present value factor defined as follows:

$$Z_t = \frac{P_{t,R} V_R}{(1+i)^{R-t}}$$

where $V_R$ is the value as of the retirement year R of $1 annuity stream starting at the retirement age and $P_{t,R}$ is the probability the employee leaves from time t to retirement date R.

Therefore, the plan level expected service cost is:

$$SC_{pt} = \sum_{a,s}\sum_n SC_{w,t}$$

where $SC_{pt}$ is Form 5500 reported expected service cost for year t, a is the age group, s is the service group and n is the number of participants in age-service group a and s.

Finally, we use the plan level service cost to estimate the benefit accrual k:

$$k = \frac{SC_{pt}}{\sum_{a,s}\sum_n SZ_t[(N_t+1)(1+i)Y_{t+1} - N_tY_t]}$$

To be clear, because we model simplified plans, the benefit factors we estimate reflect a range of plan features that affect accrual rates, not just the benefit factor themselves. These might include different COLAs, retirement ages, and vesting provisions.

b. *Salary growth (g)*. We estimate the salary growth at the plan level from the time series of salaries for each age-service group. We weight the estimated salary growth in each age-service group by the number of participants.

Table III reports plan-reported discount rates and the calibration results. It is worth noting that the use of market-based discount rates assumes that the bond market properly prices the risk of future inflation. This is particularly true if there are gaps between when workers separate from employment and when they begin drawing a pension. If inflation turns out to be much higher than expected, then the nominal benefit in the DB plan ends up being cheap for the sponsor. The benefit for those who separate from employment before drawing the pension is eroded by the inflation, and this is particularly the case for employees who won't draw benefits for a long time. In contrast, if inflation turns out to be unexpectedly low, then the nominal benefit promised in the DB ends up being very expensive for the sponsor, both because of less erosion of the benefits for separated employees and a higher duration of the promised cash flows.[11] Our assumption is that market discount rates correctly price the risks of future inflation.

The average salary growth varies from 3.35% in 2000 to 4.76% in 2002, but we observe a significant cross sectional variation in all years from about -1.20% to 11.2%. Similarly, the calibrated benefit factor varies from 0% to 4% across plans and years, with a mean of 1.17% and a median of 1.06%. We winsorize both variables at the 0.01 level to reduce the impact of any extreme outliers. Figure 1 reports distribution of the estimated benefit factor. We note a significant mass around zero, as firms that freeze will have no benefit accrual in the years following the freeze. Nevertheless, we find that not all frozen plan report zero benefit accruals. Some of them carry forward a small group of grandfathered participants, in which case, the plan would still report a positive expected service cost even if frozen.

## 2.3. Measurement of Accruals

In the absence of any offsets, the potential cost saving from freezing plans is the value of the cost accruals that the firm would incur if the plan continued to run. The present value of accrued pension liabilities is a function of the benefit formula, the years of service of each employee, the salary of each employee, and the present value of an annuity beginning in each employee's retirement year. The expected cost accruals are simply the expected change in the present value of the liability in the absence of a freeze.

---

[11] We thank Stan Panis for highlighting this point.

These potential accruals could in theory be measured over a window of any length of time. Suppose the firm is considering a freeze at time $t$. The accumulated benefit obligation (ABO) liability for one worker at time $s>t$ if the plan is not frozen will be calculated as follows:

$$ABO_{s|[no\ freeze\ at\ t]} = kN_sY_s\left[\frac{P_{s,R}V_R}{(1+i)^{R-s}}\right] = kN_sY_sZ_s$$

where $k$ is the benefit factor, $N_s$ is the number of years in service, $Y_s$ is the salary and the bracketed term is the discount factor $Z_s$ we defined earlier. However, if the freeze is implemented, the number of years in service and the salary will remain the same. Therefore, the accumulated benefit obligation will be:

$$ABO_{s|[freeze\ at\ t]} = kN_tY_t\left[\frac{P_{s,R}V_R}{(1+i)^{R-s}}\right] = kN_t\,Y_t\,Z_s$$

At time $t$, the additional benefit earned by one worker in the absence of a plan freeze will be:

$$\delta_t = (ABO_{s|[no\ freeze\ at\ t]} - ABO_{s|[freeze\ at\ t]})(1+i)^{-(s-t)}$$

or

$$\delta_t = kZ_t[(N_s - N_t)Y_s + (Y_s - Y_t)N_t]$$

In particular, if $s=t+1$ then the one year benefit accrual of one participant is:

$$\delta_t = kZ_tY_t\left[1 + \left(\frac{Y_{t+1}-Y_t}{Y_t}\right)(N_t+1)\right] = kZ_tY_t[1 + g(N_t+1)]$$

Similarly, if $s=t+5$, then the accumulated five year accrual for one participant is:

$$\delta_t = kZ_tY_t\left[5 + \left(\frac{Y_{t+1}-Y_t}{Y_t}\right)(N_t+5)\right] = kZ_tY_t[5 + g(N_t+5)]$$

Our estimation incorporates potential entry and exit into the plan in future years. In particular, the $P_{s,R}$ or the probability that a particular worker leaves the plan at time $s$ is estimated from the matrix of plan participants in consecutive years (please refer to the example available in the appendix). The separation probability for each age service group is estimated for all plans that disclose the number of participants in any year and also 5 years later, allowing us to capture a complete shift on the diagonal (down and to the right) of all participants in the group. This allows us to circumvent additional assumptions on the age service distribution of participants within each cell of the matrix. In the absence of a five year disclosure at the plan level, we use industry averages, calculated separately for freeze and non-freeze plans, for all years before the freeze. Similarly, we estimate entry rate for each age group based on the reported information in the first column of the matrix (service year less than 1), where available.

Finally, we aggregate our estimates at the age-service group level and then at the plan level. We refer to freeze plan accruals as "counterfactual" accruals because these are the accruals we estimate the plan would have experienced in the absence of the freeze.

We estimate the benefit accruals separately for cash balance plans as their benefit formula is structured differently. The cash balance increases from year to year by a certain percentage of salary and accumulated balance. We therefore require information on age-service groups account balance, in addition to participant and salary information. We estimate the cash balance increase by running a fixed plan and year effects regression of the change in the cash balance (log) on salary (log), age group and service group:

$$Log(\Delta CB)_{w,t+1} = \beta_1 + \beta_2 Age_w + \beta_3 Service_w + \beta_4 Log(Salary)_{wt} + \varepsilon_t + \vartheta_p + \delta_{wt}$$

where $\varepsilon_t$ is the time fixed effect and $\vartheta_p$ is the plan fixed effect. We then carry these balances forward by taking into account the estimated salary growth, allowing for future potential and exit into the plans as described earlier for regular plans.

Finally, our cost savings analysis requires an estimation of all future 401(k) contributions made by the sponsor after the freeze implementation. For this purpose, we aggregate all actual contributions made by the sponsor to all its 401(k) plans each year, from Form 5500 Schedule H. Next, we project what the sponsor's aggregate 401(k) contribution would have been in the absence of the DB freeze, based on estimated salary growth. Unfortunately there is no information in the 5500 for non-DB plans that would allow us to measure salary growth for participants in those plans specifically, so we assume that the rate of salary growth for existing participants in the 401(k) plan is the same as the rate of salary growth for DB plans.

We therefore multiply the actual 401(k) employer contribution before the freeze by the pre-freeze DB salary growth to calculate the projected employer 401(k) contribution in the year following the freeze, under the counterfactual assumption that the freeze did not take place. Any difference between the actual reported employer contribution and the projected employer contribution is then attributed to the accounts of the DB participants now included in these plans.

The underlying assumption behind this calculation is therefore that in the absence of the DB freeze, contributions to 401(k) plans would have grown at the rate of salary growth of 401(k) plan participants, and that this salary growth is the same as that of the DB plan participants.[12] Finally, we translate the 401(k) increases that we calculate into a present value number by using the formula of a growing annuity (over 1-10 years), in order to be consistent with the measurement of the DB accruals.

**2.4. Summary Statistics on Freeze and Non-Freeze Plans**

Panel A of Table IV shows that the freeze and non-freeze plans in our sample differ on a variety of observable dimensions. The observations in this panel consist of all traditional DB plan-years except those plan-years of freeze plans after their freeze. The pre-freeze plan-year observations on the firms that eventually freeze are pooled in the left panel, the plan-year observations on firms that do not freeze at any time in the sample are pooled in the middle panel, and the difference is presented in the right panel.

Firms that freeze pension plans are smaller in that they have an average of $22.5 billion in book assets (from Compustat) compared to $36.9 billion for non-freeze firms. They are also more levered, have lower interest coverage and smaller operating margins. The plans of firms that freeze are also smaller in that they have both fewer total participants (a difference of 4,288 at the mean and 1,126 at the median) and fewer total liabilities (by $316 million at the mean and $92 million at the median) before the freeze. Similarly, freeze plans have lower total payroll by $101 million, although their payroll is higher as a share of total assets by 3.0 percentage points. This suggests that labor costs are more important for firms that freeze than for firms that do not.

Freeze plans also appear to be in worse financial condition than those that do not freeze, as they have funding ratios that are on average 9% lower than non-freeze firms before the freeze. They have a higher ratio of active participants to total participants, by 5.5% at the mean and 7% at the median, implying that relatively more of the liability is coming from promises to active employees. However, freeze plans use slightly more conservative reported pension discount rates, which is interesting in light of the fact that freeze plans have a higher share of active

---

[12] To the extent that employers temporarily suspended their matching contributions after the financial crisis (especially in 2009), our estimation overestimates the additional 401(k) contributions attributed to the transfer of DB employees into these plans.

workers than non-freeze plans. The liabilities of freeze plans are therefore longer duration and would in theory support a higher average discount rate than the non-freeze plans due to the upward sloping term structure.[13]

According to the plans' own reporting, service costs (accruals) for freeze plans are somewhat lower as a share of payroll, by around 0.9% at the mean. However, these service costs are higher as a percentage of the total liability, reflecting the fact that the total liability is smaller. This difference also implies that the ratio of payroll to total liability, and hence the expected growth rate of the total liability, is greater for the freeze plans. Based on our estimates described in the previous section, freeze firms have benefit factors that are 9 basis points greater than firms that do not freeze. Recall that the benefit factors we estimate act as a summary statistic for a range of plan features that affect accrual rates.

Panel B of Table IV compares freeze vs. non-freeze plans looking only at the sample of firms that have a cash balance feature. The observations in this panel consist of all cash balance plan-years except those of freeze plans after their freeze. Here we observe broadly similar patterns as in Panel A which considered traditional DB plans. Cash balance plans that ultimately freeze have worse funding and a higher ratio of active participants. In contrast to the relationship between freeze and non-freeze traditional DB plans, there is some evidence that the cash balance plans that ultimately freeze are at the mean somewhat larger than those that do not, though not at the median. Finally, as was the case with traditional DB plans, the cash balance plans that ultimately freeze have lower service costs as a share of payroll but higher service costs expressed as a fraction of the total liability.

## 2.5. Matched Control Samples

In order to examine whether the decision to freeze is related to accruals, we use propensity score matched control samples. The goal of this technique is to eliminate the

---

[13] One possibility is that sponsors make plans look more underfunded before the freeze in order to be able to negotiate with participants. Bounds for discount rates are set by federal regulation, but firms do have some flexibility within these bounds. For example, for 2002-2003 the current liability discount rate could not be more than 20% above or 10% below the weighted average of interest rates (set forth by the Treasury department) on the rates of interest on 30-year Treasury securities during the past 4 years. For 2004-2006, the current liability discount rate could not be 10% above or below the weighted average of interest rates on long term investment-grade corporate bonds during the previous 4 years. For 2007-2009, pursuant to the Pension Protection Act, the current liability discount rate used could not be more than 5% above or 10% below the below the weighted average of interest rates on 30-year Treasury securities during the previous 4 years.

confounding factors of unobserved industry-level trends, year-level correlations such as changes in regulation following the Pension Protection Act of 2006, and other potential covariates. Five control samples emerge from this analysis: (1) *'Non-freezes'*, the entire universe of plans that did not freeze during our sample period for which age-service tables were available; (2) *'Ind Controls'*, the subsample of the non-freezes within the same 2-digit SIC code and year; (3) *'PS Match1'*, the subsample of the non-freezes group matched on propensity scores calculated based on 2-digit SIC, ABO and year; (4) *'PS Match2'*, the subsample of the non-freezes group matched on propensity scores calculated based on 2-digit SIC, funding ratio, and year; (5) *'PS Match3'*, the subsample of the non-freezes group matched on propensity scores calculated based on 2-digit SIC, ABO, funding ratio, and year. On the presumption that industry wide trends were similar across all plans, the matched-pair research design will allow us to separate the effects of the freeze.

Our matching relies on a matching of propensity scores, originally developed by Rosenbaum and Rubin (1983, 1985) and Heckman et al. (2007). The propensity score is the conditional probability of treatment assignment given ex-ante variables. These variables include the industry classification, the accumulated benefit obligation (ABO) and the funding ratio, for the year preceding the freeze. We measure the industry at the 2-digit SIC level and the funding ratio as the difference between the pension assets and the ABO divided by the ABO. We follow a similar matching procedure to identify matched plans for CB plans freezes from a large sample of CB plans that did not freeze during our sample period.

Our final treatment sample includes 116 traditional pension freezes and 49 cash balance freezes. Our control groups have 4,896 non-freeze plans, 1,634 industry control plans, and 116 PS Matched plans. Similarly, we identify 1,641 non-freeze cash balance plans, 338 cash balance industry control plans and 49 PS Matched cash balance plans.

## 3. Results
### 3.1. Estimated Cost Savings

The first question we address is whether firms that freeze their DB plans achieve cost savings. In freezing a DB plan, a firm stops DB accruals completely. However, after the freeze, employers generally contribute to DC plans for the employees. If the employer ultimately increases DC contributions by as much as (or more than) the DB accruals would have been, then the firm does not save any costs.

Table V shows counterfactual DB accruals and estimated actual increases in 401(k) contributions as a share of payroll, for both firms that freeze traditional DB plans and those that freeze cash balance plans. This analysis is conducted at sponsor firm level. The difference between counterfactual DB accruals and actual DC contribution increases represents the cost savings realized by the firm, assuming that there are no other offsets to the employees such as improvements in non-pension fringe benefits. (We address the possibility of compensating salary changes later.)

The top row of Table V shows the counterfactual accruals over time horizons ranging from one to ten years. Whether the per-year accrual is expected to be increasing or decreasing with the time horizon depends on several factors. First, due to the interaction between salary and years of service, accrual patterns in DB plans for a given employee are typically convex with respect to his age, so that an $n$-year accrual for a given employee more than $n$ times a one-year accrual. However, an employee who is going to retire or leave the firm in the near future has no accruals beyond this date, and thus long-horizon accruals for older workers may not be as large as those of younger workers, a possibility we investigate below. Workers with around or just over $n$ (e.g. 10) years of work remaining would have the highest expected accruals over those $n$ years (e.g. 10 years). The age and service distribution of workers within a plan along with entry and exit and the benefit accrual slopes of those individual workers, will in aggregate determine the convexity of the plan's total benefit accrual with respect to time.

The first row of Table V shows the projected counterfactual accrual for horizons of one to ten years for the freeze firms in the sample. These are the average accruals to workers in the plans that would be accrued if the plans did not freeze. The table shows that the accruals are slightly concave with respect to the horizon for the first five years, and then becomes even more concave as workers with fewer than ten years remaining retire.[14] For instance, average accruals between year 1 and year 5 are below our estimated accruals (for example, 6.25% + (29.02%-

---

[14] The separating probability from the plan is integrated for all future years and for all age service groups. Our estimation is not able to differentiate between participants who retire or leave the firm. However, the exit probability for older and longer tenured probability is most likely due to retirement. Benefits earned by workers that exit the plan before the year of the estimation are also incorporated, up to the year of separation. Entry in future years and the benefits earned by these employees thereafter are included as well.

6.25%) * 0.25 = 11.9% which is smaller than 12.32%). As we will show momentarily, this pattern is due to the fact that over longer horizons, older workers are retiring and therefore would only have accrued benefits for a limited number of years.

The second row of Table V shows the estimated actual increases in contributions to 401(k) plans as a share of payroll. These are also slightly concave, which is related to the fact that discount rates are generally higher than salary growth.[15] Recall that these long-run estimates of DC contributions are based on the assumption that the DB participants of the frozen plan are offered a 401(k) alternative and any additional contribution into these plans (in excess of their normal growth) must be originated by these new participants. Compared to a one-year counterfactual DB accrual of 6.2% of payroll, we find that firms increase contributions to DC plans by 2.6% of payroll in the first year after the freeze. Over 10 years, compared to counterfactual DB accruals of 54% of payroll, we estimate that firms will contribute approximately 23% of payroll.[16]

The *Difference* line in Table V shows the difference between counterfactual accruals and estimated actual 401(k) contribution increases.[17] The *Break even condition* line in the table then shows the annualized, compound additional yearly pre-tax compensation as a percentage of payroll that would be required as a supplement to the post-freeze pension benefit in order to equalize compensation before and after the freeze. There is a shortfall from the perspective of the employee (and thus cost savings from the perspective of the firm) of 3.6% of payroll over a one-year horizon, and 30.1% of payroll over a 10-year horizon. Alternatively, the employee would need a 2.7% compounded annual increase in pre-tax compensation to be indifferent over 10 years.[18]

---

[15] As explained in Section 2.3, the 401(k) increases are converted to a present value in order to be consistent with the measurement of the DB accruals.

[16] Our estimates are in effect very close to those reported by Towers Watson in 2009 in their report on "Employer Commitment to Retirement Plans in the United States" (Towers Watson (2009)). Although their data sources and analysis is very different from ours, they find that "sponsors that transitioned from DB to DC-only coverage increased their DC benefits values by an average of 27 percentage points (of payroll), but the enhancement covered only about half of the DB value lost by closing or freezing pension plans".

[17] While the administrative costs might be different under the two arrangements, current evidence is inconclusive. Administrative expenses are frequently paid by plan participants in DC arrangements. New disclosures on such fees and expenses would be available to participants under Department of Labor regulations by the end of 2012.

[18] The additional compensation would only have to be pre-tax as the counterfactual DB benefit payments would be taxed, and hence the DB accruals are analogous to pre-tax income.

These results can be interpreted in several contexts. Workers as a group would have to value the structure, choice, flexibility, or portability of DC plans by at least 2.7-3.6% of payroll to experience welfare gains from freezes. From the perspective of the firm, on the other hand, it appears substantial cost savings are realized from freezes. The bottom of Table V shows the same analysis scaled by total firm assets to illustrate the financial impact on the firm. The difference between forgone accruals and new firm contributions to DC plans is 0.40% of firm assets in the first year, and 3.1% of total firm assets over 10 years.

Panel B shows that for cash balance plans, both the counterfactual accruals and the estimated 401(k) increases are significantly smaller. Nevertheless, the net shortfalls from the perspective of the employee (and thus cost savings from the perspective of the firm) are quite similar to the cost effects of the DB plan freezes. Specifically, meeting the break even condition would require extra pre-tax pay of 2.51% of payroll over a 1-year horizon and 24.6% of payroll over a 10-year horizon, or 2.23% pay increases compounded annually over 10 years.

In Figure 2, we investigate the extent to which the cost savings is greater for certain age groups. The graph in the upper left shows the accruals for the freeze plans by age group, scaled by payroll, and the graph in the lower left shows the same accruals scaled by plan assets. At a 5-year horizon the youngest group would have had accruals of 2% of payroll, the middle group of 12% of payroll, and the oldest group 16% of payroll, for a total of 30% which closely matches the 5-year accruals shown in Table V.[19] Over a 10-year horizon, the workers who were 20-34 at the time of the freeze have accruals of 4% of payroll, the workers who were 35-49 at the time of the freeze have accruals of 23% payroll, and the workers who were over 50 have accruals of 27% payroll, totaling the 54% of payroll shown in Table V.

Relative to the projected increase in 401(k) contributions for these plans, the figures on the right then show that for the youngest employees (ages 20-34), the increased 401(k) contributions mostly offset the lost DB accruals.[20] On a horizon of one to five-seven years, the most savings is achieved at the expense of the workers in the oldest age group (ages 50-65), followed by those in the middle group (ages 35-49). On a horizon of longer than seven years, the

---

[19] Very small differences from Table V are due to fact that ratios are averaged here by cohort and not across all plans.
[20] As expected, savings are negative in the near future for the youngest cohorts, as their accumulated benefits tend to be small. Note that the smaller magnitudes in the graph reflect the cumulative net savings per groups at the plan level and therefore the fact that the younger cohorts have a smaller number of participants.

middle group (ages 35-39) bears the greatest cost as a share of payroll. For example, over 10 years, for employees aged 35-49, there is a difference of approximately 17.1% of payroll and for employees aged 50-65 there is a difference of 15% of payroll. The total cost savings for firms (30.7% of payroll as reported in Table V) is therefore achieved due to the fact that the increase in DC contributions is small relative to the forgone DB accruals for workers in the 35-65 age range, and especially in the 35-49 age range. As a share of firm assets (and for cash balance plan freezes, which are not shown in the graphs) the patterns are similar.

Overall, workers would have to value the structure, choice, flexibility, or portability of DC plans by at least 2.7-3.6% of payroll per year in order not to receive welfare losses from freezes of traditional DB and cash balance plans.

## 3.2. Accrual Comparison

In this section we address the question of whether plans that freeze would have experienced higher or lower accruals than comparable plans that do not freeze. Table VI compares the counterfactual projected accruals of freeze plans with the projected accruals of non-freeze plans over horizons from one to ten years. We focus on scaling by total firm assets, as this reflects the fact that the firm cares about the cost savings of the freeze compared to the total value of the firm rather than just relative to payroll.

Table VI presents the projected DB accruals for freeze firms and for various possible control samples. The top row is the same calculation as in Table V, except that the analysis here is at the plan level and not aggregated at the sponsor level. In the next row, we show the accruals for all non-freeze firms. For these firms, DB pension accruals are around 37% lower than freeze firms on a one-year horizon (0.26% of assets compared to 0.41% of assets) and even lower at longer horizons. The difference between counterfactual freeze and projected non-freeze firm accruals amounts to 0.15% (=0.0041-0.0026) of assets at a one-year horizon and 1.00% (=0.0335-0.0239) of assets at a ten-year horizon. These differences are statistically significant at the 1% level. Restricting the control sample to the plans that are in the same SIC2 industry and year as the freeze plans yields very similar results. Thus, firms that actually freeze have greater potential cost savings from accruals than the firms that do not freeze.

However, as shown in the comparison of means in Table IV, plans that freeze are different from plans that do not freeze in meaningful ways. Most critically, they are smaller in terms of total liabilities, and they also have lower funding ratios. The *PS Match* lines in Table V show the counterfactual freeze plan accruals relative to the projected accruals of propensity-score matched firms that do not freeze. The first propensity score matched sample (PS1) is matched on industry, year, and total size of the accrued liability. These second propensity score matched sample (PS2) is matched on industry, year, and funding ratio. The third propensity score matched sample (PS3) matches on industry, year, total size of accrued liability, and funding ratio. The accruals of the propensity score matched sample are in almost all cases slightly lower than the accruals of the larger and more general control samples. Overall, comparing the estimated counterfactual accruals of the freeze plans to the estimated accruals of the PS Matched control plans yields very similar results to the differences we find when we use the larger and more general control samples.

Panel B of Table VI makes similar calculations for the freeze and control samples of cash balance plans and finds similar patterns. For example, the difference between counterfactual freeze and projected non-freeze cash balance accruals amounts to 0.08% (=0.0026-0.0018) of assets at a one-year horizon and 0.7% (=0.0247-0.0177) of assets at a ten-year horizon.

In untabulated results we also examined these relationships for accruals as a share of payroll. Under this scaling the differences are typically only statistically significant in propensity score matched samples, reflecting the differences in the relative magnitudes of payroll and assets for the freeze and non-freeze samples. As shown in Table IV, payroll is a considerably larger share of total assets for freeze firms than non-freeze firms. The difference in accruals as a share of total assets is therefore in part due to the fact that firms that freeze have relatively larger payrolls, and in part due to the different age-service distributions and plan parameters (higher benefit factors and salary growth) of the freeze firms.

Figure 3 illustrates these patterns graphically, where the most relevant comparison is the solid line (freeze sample) to the dotted line (matched controls). The upper left graph shows projected counterfactual benefit accruals for freeze plans relative to projected benefit accruals for non-freeze plans, scaled by total assets. The lower left graph does the same for cash balance plans. These correspond directly to the top and bottom panels of Table VI respectively. The graph on the right show that when scaling by total payroll, both the unmatched and the matched sample of non-freeze firms have larger accruals as a share of payroll than the freeze firms, but these differences are insignificant.

Figure 4 examines one potential explanation for why freeze and non-freeze plans may differ in their accruals, specifically the age and service distribution of the workforce. The left column of graphs shows the age and service distribution of freeze and non-freeze plans. As in Tables V and VI, when calculating the statistics for the freeze firms we include only those observations in years before the freeze. From the graph in the upper left, it can be seen that plans that ultimately freeze have more workers ages 55-64 and fewer workers ages 40-54 than comparable firms that do not freeze. Specifically, around 2% less of the workforce is 40-44 years old, around 1.5% less of the workforce is 45-49 years old, around 2% more of the workforce is 55-59, and around 1% more of the workforce is 60-64. Service patterns are similar but more extreme. Freeze plans having a lower share of workers with 5-29 years of service, but a higher share of very long-tenured employees with 30 years or more service. The graphs on the right show the similar comparisons limiting the control group to the propensity score matched sample. In Figure 5, the joint age-service distribution is shown for freeze plans (Panel A), non-freeze plans (Panel B), and the difference between the two (Panel C). Freeze firms appear to have a small mountain of older and longer-tenured workers.

Motivated by these patterns, we examine whether the accrual differences between freeze plans and propensity-score matched control firms are driven by accrual differences for older employees. As was shown in Figure 2 and discussed previously, the most cost savings over the first 5 years comes from the highest age group, but the most savings over a 5-10 year horizon comes from the middle age group. Figure 6 shows the projected benefit accruals for freeze plans for the three age groups (20-34, 35-49, and 50-65) relative to the propensity-score matched control plans and finds similar patterns. Over all years, the largest difference in benefit accruals comes from the older workers (who are over-represented in the freeze plans), although the difference becomes smaller for the 5-10 year horizon. This analysis indicates that while the differential demographics of the freeze and non-freeze plans likely plays a role in the accrual differences, it is not the only factor. Figure 6 clearly shows that in all of the age groups the freeze plans have higher accruals than the control firms.

Table VII undertakes a more precise decomposition of the accrual differences for freeze and non-freeze firms into benefit-related parameters, demographic factors, and the size of the labor force relative to firm assets. In each panel, the starting point is the counterfactual prospective DB accruals for freeze firms. The characteristics of each firm are then replaced with those of the propensity score matched controls sequentially and cumulatively, and the prospective DB accruals are re-calculated.

The results are independent upon the particular propensity score control sample used. In all cases, scaling by total sponsor assets and the relative ratio of participants to assets ratio has a substantial effect on accruals. For example, in the *PS Match1* the combined effect decreases accruals from 0.0041 to 0.0031, almost half of the differential accruals between the freeze plans and their matched sample. This suggests that labor is more important in the firm production function for sponsors that freeze their plans versus those who do not.

The plan age-service distribution of participants (demographics) and salaries (human capital) have a further effect of decreasing the difference in accruals by about 21% ( that is (0.0031-0.0027)/(0.0041-0.0022)). The remaining difference of about 26% is attributed to the combined effect of plan level assumptions on the benefit formulas (the benefit accrual, salary growth and the discount factor). Of all, probably the most significant effect comes from the larger benefit factor offered by freeze plans sponsors to their employees).

Table VIII shows probit analysis of accruals on the probability of freezing. The dependent variable is 1 if the plan is frozen in the following year and zero otherwise. Plan-year observations after the plan has been frozen are excluded, and all standard errors are clustered at the firm level. The first column shows that firms with higher accruals as a share of total firm assets (*dABO/TA*) are more likely to freeze, controlling for the size of the plan. The marginal effect is 2.06, which implies that for each 1 percentage point increase in DB accruals scaled by total assets, there is a 2.06 percentage point higher probability of the plan freezing. One standard deviation of dABO/TA is 0.4%, so a plan with on standard deviation more accruals is 0.82 (=0.4*2.06) percentage points more likely to be frozen.

The remaining columns of Table VIII include controls for various other plan characteristics. The greater the share of active participants in the plan, the more likely the plan is to freeze. Plans with higher funding levels are less likely to freeze, and plans with unionized workforces are less likely to freeze. Measures of the financial health of the firm such as margins and interest coverage do not have strong effects in the presence of the accruals variable. In the most restrictive specifications, a 1 percentage point increase in DB accruals scaled by total assets is correlated with a 1.147 percentage point higher probability of a plan freeze.

### 3.3. Salary Growth

In Table IX we examine whether there is a compensating differential through salary increases after freezes. In fact we find the opposite. There are 72 plan-year freeze observations for which salary data exist in at least one year before the freeze and one year after the freeze. Before the freeze, employees these plans see average salary growth of 4.35%, but the year after the freeze salary only grows by an average 2.56%. Control firms see comparable salary growth in years before the freeze and substantially higher salary growth in the year after the freeze. For example, the PS1 group matched to the freezes on industry, year, and size of liability sees average salary growth of 4.44% in the years before the freeze and 5.72% in the year after the freeze. The PS3 group matched to the freezes on industry, year, size of liability, and funding ratio, sees slightly lower salary growth in the years before the matched firm conducts the freeze (4.07%), but 5.31% salary growth after the freeze.

The evolution of salaries in the control plans also allows us to address some alternative hypotheses about cost saving, specifically that the cost saving we observe might simply reflect other labor cost saving measures that would have been taken in the absence of a freeze. In other words, if firms that freeze are distressed or need to cut labor costs, they might have faced a choice between either freezing the plan or directly cutting wages, and then the cost savings measured in Section 3.1 above would not be cost saving from the freeze but rather a measure of general compensation cuts that are achieved by distressed firms. However, in Table IX where we examine the salary changes of propensity-score matched firms, we find that in fact firms in the same industry and year with similar pension funding ratios actually had higher salary growth rates than the firms that did freeze their plans. To the extent that a deteriorated funding ratio is an indication of the sponsor's weak financial condition, these results suggest that employers of similar financial condition that decided not to freeze their pension plans did not elect to cut wage compensation instead.

## 4. Conclusions

This paper establishes that firms that have frozen pension plans have reduced their costs of providing retirement benefits to workers even net of increases to 401(k) contributions over horizons ranging from one to ten years. Employees of these firms, on the other hand, have seen decreases in the net present value of their retirement benefits, again inclusive of increases to 401(k) plans. Furthermore, we find that firms that have potentially more cost savings to gain by freezing plans are more likely to undertake pension freezes.

Since the marginal product of labor is unlikely to fall discretely upon a pension freeze, these results imply a change in the present value of employee compensation relative to the marginal product of labor inputs. This finding raises several questions for future research. First, whether workers are actually made worse off by these changes depends on whether they have substantial preferences for DC benefits over DB. Further investigations into worker preferences about the form of retirement benefits are required to determine the welfare impact of freezes on employees. Second, it is important to understand whether pension freezes are bringing employee compensation more in line with their marginal product or moving it further away. If freezes represent the ability of employers to seize rents through bargaining power, the implications for economic efficiency are quite different than if they represent the ability of employers to restore balance between compensation and marginal product. Third, while we have demonstrated a strong correlation between accruals and the probability of freezing a pension plan, there are still many other factors that enter a firm's decision to freeze, including the impact on the volatility of cash flows, the demand of employees for more portable benefits, and the relative effects of the two types of plans on reported accounting income. The relative importance of these effects compared to the desire to save costs remains an open question.

# REFERENCES

Aaronson, S. and J. Coronado, 2005, Are Firms Or Workers Behind the Shift Away from DB Pension Plan?, Finance and Economics Discussion Series 2005-17, Board of Governors of the Federal Reserve System (U.S.).

Ballester, M., D. Fried, and J. Livnat, 2002, Pension Plan Contributions And Financial Slack, Working Paper, New York University.

Beaudoin, C. A., Chandar, N. and E.W. Werner, 2010, Are Potential Effects Of SFAS 158 Associated With Firms' Decisions To Freeze Their Defined Benefit Pension Plans, *Review of Accounting and Finance* 9, 424-451.

Belt, B., 2005, Testimony before the Committee on education and the workforce, United States House Of Representatives.

Bergstresser, D., M. A. Desai, and J. Rauh, 2006, Earnings Manipulation, Pension Assumptions And Managerial Investment Decisions, *Quarterly Journal Of Economics* 121(1), 157-195

Black, F., 1980, The Tax Consequences Of Long-Run Pension Policy, *Financial Analyst Journal*, 36 (4), 21-28.

Bodie, Z., Alan J.M., and R.C. Merton, 1988, Defined Benefit versus Defined Contribution Pension Plans: What are the Real Trade-offs?, NBER Chapters, in: Pensions in the U.S. Economy, 139-162, National Bureau of Economic Research, Inc.

Buessing, Marric, and Mauricio Soto, 2006, The State Of Private Pensions: Current 5500 Data, Center For Retirement Research Issue In Brief 42.

Clark, Robert, and Ann McDermed, 1990, *The Choice Of Pension Plans In A Changing Environment*. Washington: American Enterprise Institute.

Cocco, J. And Volpin, 2007, The Corporate Governance Of Defined Benefit Pension Plans: Evidence From The United Kingdom", *Financial Analysts Journal* 63, 70-83.

Friedberg, L. and M. Owyang, 2004, Explaining The Evolution Of Pension Structure And Job Tenure, NBER Working Paper #10714.

Friedberg, L., M. Owyang, and T.Sinclair, 2006, Searching For Better Prospects: Endogenizing Falling Job Tenure And Private Pension Coverage, Topics In Economic Analysis And Policy 6(1).

Gustman, Alan, And Thomas Steinmeier, 1992, The Stampede Towards Defined Contribution Plans, *Industrial Relations* 31, 361-369.

Heckman, J. and E.J. Vytlacil, 2007, Econometric Evaluation Of Social Programs, Part I : Causal Models, Structural Models And Econometric Policy Evaluation, *Handbook Of Econometrics* 6B, ed. J. Heckman and E. Leamer. Amsterdam: Elsevier, 4779-4874

Ippolito, R. A., 1985, The Economic Function Of Underfunded Pension Plans, *Journal Of Law And Economics* 28, 611-651.

Ippolito, Richard A., And John W. Thompson, 2000, The Survival Rate Of Defined Benefit Plans, 1987-1995, *Industrial Relations* 39, 228-245.

Kruse, Douglas, 1995, Pension Substitution In The 1980s: Why The Shift Toward Defined Contribution Plans, *Industrial Relations* 34, 218-241.

Lazear, E. 1979, Why Is There Mandatory Retirement? *The Journal Of Political Economy* 6, 1261-1284

Lazear, E., 1983, "Pensions as Severance Pay," in *Financial Aspects of the United States Pension System*, Z. Bodie and J. Shoven, eds., Chicago: University of Chicago Press, 57-89.

Lazear, E.P. and R.L. Moore, 1988, Pensions and turnover. In Pensions inthe US. economy, ed. Zvi Bodie, John B. Shoven, and David A. Wise, 163-88, Chicago: University of Chicago Press.

McFarland, P. and M. Warshawsky, 2009, Does Freezing a Defined-Benefit Pension Plan Increase Company Value? Empirical Evidence, *Financial Analysts Journal* 65(4), 47-59.

Milevsky, M. and K. Song, 2010, Do Markets Like Frozen Defined Benefit Pension Plans? An Event Study, *Journal of Risk and Insurance* 77(4), 893-909.

Mitchell, O.S. and G.S. Fields, 1984, The economics of retirement behavior, *Journal of Labor Economics* 42(1), 84-105.

Munnell, A.H. and M. Soto, 2007, Why Are Companies Freezing Their Pensions?, Center For Retirement Research At Boston College, working paper 2007-22,

Morgensen, G., 2011, Dear Committee: Main Street Says Look at Pensions, *New York Times*, 12 November 2011.

Petersen, M. A., 1992. Pension Reversions And Worker-Stockholder Wealth Transfers, *The Quarterly Journal Of Economics* 107(3), 1033-56.

Petersen, M. A., 1994, Cashflow Variability and Firm's Pension Choice: A Role for Operating Leverage, *Journal of Financial Economics* 36, 361-383.

Poterba J, J. Rauh, S. Venti, and D. Wise, 2007, Defined Contribution Plans, Defined Benefit Plans, and the Accumulation of Retirement Wealth, *Journal of Public Economics* 91(10), 2062-2086.

Rauh, J., 2006, Investment and Financing Constraints: Evidence From The Funding Of Corporate Pension Plans, *Journal Of Finance* 61(1), 33-71.

Rosenbaum, P. R., and D. B. Rubin, 1985, Constructing a Control Group Using Multivariate Matched Sampling Methods That Incorporate the Propensity Score. *The American Statistician* 39, 33-38.

Shapiro, C. and Stiglitz, J.E., 1984, Equilibrium Unemployment As A Worker Disci-Pline Device, *American Economic Review*, 74, 433-44.

Shivdasani, A. and Stefanescu, I., 2010, How do pensions plans affect capital structure decisions?, *The Review of Financial Studies*, 23, 1287-1323.

Rubin, J., 2007, The Impact of Pension Freezes on Firm Value, University of Pennsylvania, working paper.

Samwick, A.A. and J. Skinner, 2004, Will 401(k) Pension Plans Affect Retirement Income?, *The American Economic Review*, 94(1), 329-343.

Stock, J.H., and D.A. Wise, 1990, Pensions, The Option Value of Work, and Retirement, *Econometrics* 58(5), 1151-1180.

Tepper, I., 1981, Taxation and Corporate Pension Policy, *Journal of Finance* 36 (1), 1-13.Towers Watson, 2009, Employer Commitment to Retirement Plans in the United States.

Towers Watson, 2011, Pension Freezes Among the Fortune 1000 in 2011.

Towers Watson, 2012, Pensions in transition: Retirement Plan Changes and Employer Motivations.

Vanderhei, Jack, 2006, EBRI Issue In Brief #291, Employee Benefits Research Institute.

## Table I: Sample Selection of Defined Benefit Plans

This table describes our sample selection process. First, we identify all defined benefit plans filing Form 5500 with the Internal Revenue Service and the Department of Labor (column 1). Second, we extract the subset of plans sponsored by companies covered by Compustat (column 2). Our methodology requires the disclosure of the age-service matrix, which is only mandated for plans with more than 1000 active participants. We therefore restrict the sample based on whether the plan reported more than 1000 active participants for at least one year during our sample period (column 3). The age-service matrix is disclosed in the attachments to Form 5500. We screen our sample for the availability of such attachments (column 4). We manually search these filings for the age-service matrices which contain participants and salary information. We report the number of plans for which participant information is available in column 5. For confidentiality purposes, the salary information is only disclosed for cells with more than 20 participants. We report the number of plans for which salary information exists in column 6. As a first screen test, we identify hard freezes based on the plan disclosure from Form 5500 (column 7). Separately, we identify all defined benefit plans that disclose a cash balance feature (column 8). When these plans disclose a cash balance table in the attachments, we report it in column 9.

| Fiscal Year | Universe | Linked to Compustat | w/ at least 1000 active | w/ attachments | w/ participants table | w/ salary table | w/ Hard Freeze Code | w/CBP code | w/ cash balance table |
|---|---|---|---|---|---|---|---|---|---|
| | (1) | (2) | (3) | (4) | (5) | (6) | (7) | (8) | (9) |
| 1999 | 27,733 | 3335 | 1,061 | 45 | 45 | 35 | 0 | 5 | 0 |
| 2000 | 39,270 | 4311 | 1,386 | 22 | 17 | 15 | 0 | 5 | 0 |
| 2001 | 40,984 | 4284 | 1,413 | 42 | 28 | 22 | 0 | 6 | 0 |
| 2002 | 40,904 | 4065 | 1,380 | 51 | 51 | 43 | 3 | 10 | 0 |
| 2003 | 41,171 | 3912 | 1,373 | 1,228 | 1,205 | 925 | 53 | 271 | 214 |
| 2004 | 41,285 | 3729 | 1,333 | 1,296 | 1,274 | 988 | 73 | 291 | 260 |
| 2005 | 41,981 | 3745 | 1,342 | 1,322 | 1,307 | 991 | 100 | 313 | 270 |
| 2006 | 42,413 | 3604 | 1,321 | 1,238 | 1,197 | 862 | 126 | 284 | 251 |
| 2007 | 42,609 | 3429 | 1,286 | 1,175 | 1,137 | 780 | 159 | 292 | 255 |
| 2008 | 47,376 | 3092 | 1,197 | 935 | 906 | 614 | 167 | 233 | 211 |
| 2009 | 36,639 | 2605 | 1,055 | 1,044 | 1,035 | 705 | 189 | 307 | 265 |
| 2010 | 17,208 | 526 | 168 | 153 | 147 | 88 | 27 | 32 | 27 |
| 2011 | 13 | | | | | | | | |
| Total | 459,586 | 40,637 | 14,315 | 8,551 | 8,349 | 6,068 | 897 | 2,049 | 1,753 |

## TABLE II: Sample Freezes

This table describes the sample selection of defined benefit plans (DBPs) subject to a hard freeze during our sample period. A hard freeze implies the plan closure to new participants and the discontinuation of all benefit accruals. While hard freezes are reported in Form 5500, often the disclosure is delayed. We proceed by manually searching the news and the attachments to Form 5500 in order to correctly identify the year of the freeze. In column 1 we report the plans that froze during our sample period and the year of the freeze. In column 2 we report the plans for which we could identify at least one attachment to form 5500 prior to the freeze. In columns 3-4 we report the availability of the age-service matrix for regular freezes, while in columns 5-7 we report the availability of the age-service matrix for cash balance plans. Cash balance plans (CBPs) are defined benefit plans for accounting and funding purposes. However, the benefit accrual is calculated based on a different rule.

| Fiscal Year | Freeze Year Hand collected | Freezes with PDF attachments before freeze | DBPs with participants table | DBPs w/salary table | CBPs with participants table | CBPs with salary table | CBPs with account balance table |
|---|---|---|---|---|---|---|---|
| | (1) | (2) | (3) | (4) | (5) | (6) | (7) |
| 2000 | 2 | | | | | | |
| 2001 | 7 | | | | | | |
| 2002 | 14 | 2 | 2 | 1 | | | |
| 2003 | 25 | 15 | 12 | 12 | 3 | 2 | |
| 2004 | 25 | 22 | 15 | 10 | 7 | 5 | 5 |
| 2005 | 21 | 18 | 13 | 13 | 5 | 4 | 2 |
| 2006 | 33 | 33 | 23 | 21 | 10 | 9 | 9 |
| 2007 | 27 | 26 | 21 | 18 | 5 | 2 | 2 |
| 2008 | 21 | 21 | 14 | 12 | 7 | 7 | 6 |
| 2009 | 31 | 31 | 19 | 17 | 12 | 11 | 10 |
| 2010 | 5 | 5 | 2 | 1 | 3 | 3 | 3 |
| 2011 | 2 | 2 | 2 | 2 | | | |
| Total | 213 | 175 | 123 | 107 | 52 | 43 | 37 |

## Table III: Calibration

This table reports summary statistics of the three parameters used in the estimation of benefit accruals of active participants. The discount rate (i) is collected from Form 5500 (Schedule B). The plan level salary growth (g) is estimated based on the salary information available in the age-service matrices at cell level, across all years. For plan freezes, the estimation relies on pre-freeze years. The benefit factor (k) is also estimated as described in the text.

| Plan year | No. plans | i (MIN) | i (MED) | i (MEAN) | i (MAX) | No. plans | g (MIN) | g (MED) | g (MEAN) | g (MAX) | No. plans | k (MIN) | k (MED) | k (MEAN) | k (MAX) |
|---|---|---|---|---|---|---|---|---|---|---|---|---|---|---|---|
| 1999 | 45 | 5.62% | 6.55% | 6.37% | 6.56% | 38 | -1.21% | 4.40% | 4.31% | 11.20% | 38 | 0.00% | 1.08% | 1.05% | 4.00% |
| 2000 | 17 | 5.41% | 6.30% | 6.09% | 6.32% | 12 | -1.21% | 4.12% | 3.35% | 7.12% | 10 | 0.00% | 1.09% | 1.73% | 4.00% |
| 2001 | 28 | 5.29% | 6.21% | 6.16% | 6.23% | 21 | -1.21% | 3.82% | 3.60% | 9.54% | 21 | 0.00% | 1.55% | 1.65% | 4.00% |
| 2002 | 51 | 5.14% | 6.80% | 6.46% | 6.85% | 29 | 0.16% | 4.40% | 4.76% | 11.20% | 27 | 0.00% | 1.17% | 1.03% | 1.66% |
| 2003 | 1,204 | 4.81% | 6.65% | 6.15% | 8.18% | 1122 | -1.21% | 4.40% | 4.54% | 11.20% | 896 | 0.00% | 1.03% | 1.16% | 4.00% |
| 2004 | 1,272 | 4.72% | 6.55% | 6.39% | 8.18% | 1178 | -1.21% | 4.47% | 4.53% | 11.20% | 932 | 0.00% | 1.05% | 1.17% | 4.00% |
| 2005 | 1,306 | 4.59% | 6.10% | 6.06% | 8.18% | 1202 | -1.21% | 4.40% | 4.44% | 11.20% | 940 | 0.00% | 1.05% | 1.16% | 4.00% |
| 2006 | 1,196 | 4.60% | 5.77% | 5.72% | 8.18% | 1080 | -1.21% | 4.34% | 4.35% | 11.20% | 842 | 0.00% | 1.03% | 1.15% | 4.00% |
| 2007 | 1,136 | 5.21% | 5.78% | 5.76% | 8.02% | 1011 | -1.21% | 4.29% | 4.30% | 10.52% | 767 | 0.00% | 1.08% | 1.17% | 4.00% |
| 2008 | 905 | 5.29% | 6.12% | 6.13% | 8.25% | 794 | -1.21% | 4.25% | 4.24% | 9.89% | 606 | 0.00% | 1.08% | 1.19% | 4.00% |
| 2009 | 1,034 | 6.05% | 8.12% | 7.84% | 8.50% | 898 | -1.21% | 4.26% | 4.23% | 11.20% | 640 | 0.00% | 1.07% | 1.20% | 4.00% |
| 2010 | 147 | 5.70% | 6.64% | 6.64% | 7.61% | 132 | -1.21% | 3.96% | 4.05% | 7.98% | 103 | 0.00% | 1.13% | 1.15% | 3.95% |
| Total | 8,341 | 4.59% | 6.10% | 6.28% | 8.50% | 7,517 | -1.21% | 4.39% | 4.38% | 11.20% | 5,822 | 0.00% | 1.06% | 1.17% | 4.00% |

## Table IV: Sample Statistics

The table presents the characteristics of plans that have been frozen (for all years preceding the freeze) relative to all plans that have not been frozen. In *Panel A* we report these characteristics for freeze and non-freeze defined benefit plans while in *Panel B* we focus on defined benefit plans with a cash balance feature. *Funding (%)* is defined as plan assets minus plan liabilities divided by plan liabilities. Both plan assets and plan liabilities are collected from Form 5500. The pension liability disclosed in Form 5500 is commonly referred to as the Accumulated Benefit Obligation (ABO) and represents the present value of all accrued benefits. *Active Participants (%)* is the ratio between the number of active participants and the number of total participants, as reported in Form 5500. *Salary per active participant* is calculated based on the age-service salary information. Service cost is the reported expected increase of pension benefits during the year as reported in Form 5500. Payroll is the sum of all participants' salaries as reported in the age-service tables. Discount rate is the rate used to discount future expected pension benefits, as reported in Form 5500. The benefit factor and the salary growth are both estimated based on the collected age-service tables.

*Panel A: Frozen plans versus non-frozen plans*

|  | N | Freezes (MEAN) | Freezes (MED) | N | Non-Freezes (MEAN) | Non-Freezes (MED) | Diff (MEAN) |  | Diff (MED) |  |
| --- | --- | --- | --- | --- | --- | --- | --- | --- | --- | --- |
| *Sponsor level* | | | | | | | | | | |
| Total assets (sponsor) ($mil) | 399 | 22,545 | 2,814 | 4,897 | 36,932 | 6,664 | -14,387 | *** | -3,850 | *** |
| Market leverage | 366 | 0.34 | 0.28 | 4329 | 0.30 | 0.25 | 0.04 | ** | 0.03 | ** |
| Interest coverage | 356 | 7.64 | 4.35 | 4313 | 10.23 | 5.16 | -2.59 | ** | -0.81 | *** |
| EBITDA/Sales | 391 | 0.15 | 0.12 | 4614 | 0.17 | 0.14 | -0.02 | *** | -0.02 | *** |
| *Plan level* | | | | | | | | | | |
| ABO ($mil) | 409 | 397 | 98 | 4,981 | 713 | 189 | -316.00 | *** | -91.50 | *** |
| ABO/Total Assets (sponsor) | 399 | 10.6% | 4.8% | 4,622 | 8.1% | 3.8% | 0.02 | *** | 1.04% | *** |
| ABO / Payroll | 409 | 179.7% | 100.5% | 4,977 | 232.8% | 152.0% | -53.0% | *** | -51.5% | *** |
| Payroll ($mil) | 411 | 232 | 97 | 5,023 | 333 | 116 | -101.00 | *** | -19.50 | *** |
| Payroll/Total assets (sponsor) | 397 | 7.8% | 5.0% | 4,634 | 4.8% | 2.4% | 3.0% | *** | 2.6% | *** |
| Salary per Active Participant | 411 | 51,904 | 49,641 | 5,022 | 58,578 | 57,123 | -6,673 | *** | -7,482 | *** |
| Active Participants (%) | 407 | 55.7% | 56.6% | 4,973 | 50.2% | 49.3% | 5.5% | *** | 7.3% | *** |
| Total Participants | 409 | 9,522 | 3,671 | 4,988 | 13,810 | 4,797 | -4,288 | *** | -1,126 | *** |
| Funding (%) | 409 | -6.2% | -9.1% | 4,977 | 2.9% | -2.2% | -9.1% | *** | -6.9% | *** |
| Service Cost/ Payroll | 409 | 5.67% | 4.7% | 4,978 | 6.57% | 5.6% | -0.90% | ** | -0.81% | ** |
| Service Cost/ABO | 409 | 5.49% | 4.6% | 4,974 | 4.47% | 3.6% | 1.02% | *** | 0.98% | *** |
| Discount rate (%) | 411 | 6.15% | 6.1% | 5,022 | 6.26% | 6.1% | -0.11% | *** | 0.00% | |
| Benefit Factor (%) | 411 | 1.33% | 1.1% | 5,022 | 1.23% | 1.1% | 0.09% | *** | -0.03% | |
| Salary Growth (%) | 411 | 4.45% | 4.4% | 5,022 | 4.36% | 4.3% | 0.09% | | 0.05% | |

*Panel B: Frozen plans versus non-frozen plans (defined benefit plans with a cash balance feature)*

|  | N | CBPs Freezes (MEAN) | CBPs Freezes (MED) | N | CBPs Non-Freezes (MEAN) | CBPs Non-Freezes (MED) | Diff (MEAN) | | Diff (MED) | |
|---|---|---|---|---|---|---|---|---|---|---|
| *Sponsor level* | | | | | | | | | | |
| Total assets (sponsor) ($mil) | 171 | 45,508 | 13,365 | 1,643 | 61,558 | 11,456 | -16,050 | | 1,909 | |
| Market leverage | 144 | 0.37 | 0.31 | 1,505 | 0.33 | 0.28 | 0.04 | * | 0.03 | * |
| Interest coverage | 138 | 6.03 | 3.67 | 1,478 | 8.56 | 4.76 | -2.53 | ** | -1.09 | *** |
| EBITDA/ Sales | 159 | 0.19 | 0.15 | 1,573 | 0.20 | 0.18 | -0.01 | | -0.03 | ** |
| *Plan level* | | | | | | | | | | |
| ABO ($mil) | 170 | 2,180 | 156 | 1,688 | 1,170 | 327 | 1,010 | *** | -171 | *** |
| ABO/ Total Assets (sponsor) | 171 | 11.6% | 4.4% | 1,643 | 8.0% | 4.4% | 3.6% | *** | 0.0% | |
| ABO / Payroll | 170 | 204.5% | 79.0% | 1,688 | 241.8% | 141.9% | -37.3% | ** | -62.9% | *** |
| Payroll ($mil) | 171 | 931 | 228 | 1,689 | 597 | 245 | 334 | *** | -17 | |
| Payroll/ Total assets (sponsor) | 170 | 4.5% | 2.7% | 1,688 | 7.7% | 4.1% | -3.2% | *** | -1.4% | *** |
| Salary per Active Participant | 171 | 58,853 | 53,024 | 1,689 | 64,066 | 62,881 | -5,213 | *** | -9,857 | *** |
| Active Participants (%) | 171 | 61.1% | 62.3% | 1,689 | 54.8% | 54.9% | 6.4% | *** | 7.4% | *** |
| Total Participants | 171 | 35,844 | 9,234 | 1,689 | 23,382 | 8,787 | 12,461 | *** | 448 | *** |
| Funding (%) | 170 | -1.20% | -4.78% | 1,688 | 2.26% | 0.14% | -3.46% | *** | -4.92% | ** |
| Service Cost/ Payroll | 170 | 4.9% | 4.6% | 1,688 | 6.0% | 5.0% | -1.1% | *** | -0.4% | *** |
| Service Cost/ABO | 170 | 6.9% | 5.3% | 1,688 | 4.8% | 3.6% | 2.1% | *** | 1.6% | *** |
| Discount rate (%) | 171 | 6.1% | 6.1% | 1,689 | 6.3% | 6.1% | -0.2% | *** | 0.0% | |
| Salary Growth (%) | 171 | 4.4% | 4.2% | 1,689 | 4.2% | 4.2% | 0.2% | | 0.1% | |

## Table V: Estimated Cost Savings as a Share of Payroll at the Sponsor Level

The table presents the estimated cost savings emerging from pension plan freezes, at sponsor level. Panel A focuses on regular freezes whereas Panel B focuses on cash balance plan freezes. *Payroll* is the sum of all participants' salaries for the year preceding the estimation. *Assets* denotes the total book assets of the sponsoring firm. *dABO* is the estimated benefit accrual for regular plans, aggregated at the sponsor level. *dCashBalance* is the estimated benefit accrual for cash balance plans, aggregated at the sponsor level. *d401k* is the increase in the 401(k) contribution following the freeze. *Difference* is the difference between the dABO and d401(k) lines. The *Break even condition* is the compounded annualized pre-tax compensation increase that would make the pension benefit in the absence of the freeze equal to the pension benefit in the presence of the freeze.

*Panel A: Defined Benefit Plan Freezes*

| | N | Year 1 | Year 2 | Year 3 | Year 4 | Year 5 | Year 6 | Year 7 | Year 8 | Year 9 | Year 10 |
|---|---|---|---|---|---|---|---|---|---|---|---|
| dABO/ payroll [counterfactual] | 114 | 0.0625 | 0.1232 | 0.1815 | 0.2379 | 0.2902 | 0.3589 | 0.4091 | 0.4573 | 0.5023 | 0.5434 |
| d401k/ payroll [estimated actual] | 114 | 0.0262 | 0.0519 | 0.0768 | 0.1013 | 0.1251 | 0.1484 | 0.1711 | 0.1934 | 0.2152 | 0.2365 |
| Difference | | 0.036 | 0.071 | 0.105 | 0.137 | 0.165 | 0.211 | 0.238 | 0.264 | 0.287 | 0.307 |
| Break even condition | | 3.63% | 3.50% | 3.37% | 3.25% | 3.10% | 3.24% | 3.10% | 2.97% | 2.84% | 2.71% |
| dABO/ TA [counterfactual] | 114 | 0.0044 | 0.0085 | 0.0125 | 0.0161 | 0.0195 | 0.024 | 0.0271 | 0.0301 | 0.0329 | 0.0353 |
| d401k/ TA [estimated actual] | 114 | 0.0005 | 0.0009 | 0.0014 | 0.0018 | 0.0022 | 0.0027 | 0.003 | 0.0034 | 0.0038 | 0.0042 |
| Difference | | 0.004 | 0.008 | 0.011 | 0.014 | 0.017 | 0.021 | 0.024 | 0.027 | 0.029 | 0.031 |
| Break even condition | | 0.39% | 0.38% | 0.37% | 0.36% | 0.34% | 0.35% | 0.34% | 0.33% | 0.32% | 0.31% |

*Panel B: Cash Balance Plan Freezes*

|  | N | Year 1 | Year 2 | Year 3 | Year 4 | Year 5 | Year 6 | Year 7 | Year 8 | Year 9 | Year 10 |
|---|---|---|---|---|---|---|---|---|---|---|---|
| dCB/ payroll [counterfactual] | 45 | 0.0275 | 0.0549 | 0.082 | 0.1088 | 0.1348 | 0.1618 | 0.189 | 0.2162 | 0.2433 | 0.2686 |
| d401k/ payroll [estimated actual] | 45 | 0.0024 | 0.0047 | 0.007 | 0.0093 | 0.0115 | 0.0137 | 0.0159 | 0.018 | 0.0201 | 0.0222 |
| Difference |  | 0.025 | 0.050 | 0.075 | 0.100 | 0.123 | 0.148 | 0.173 | 0.198 | 0.223 | 0.246 |
| Break even condition |  | 2.51% | 2.48% | 2.44% | 2.40% | 2.35% | 2.33% | 2.31% | 2.29% | 2.26% | 2.23% |
| dCB/TA [counterfactual] | 45 | 0.0026 | 0.0053 | 0.0079 | 0.0104 | 0.0130 | 0.0155 | 0.0180 | 0.0205 | 0.0229 | 0.0254 |
| d401k/ TA [estimated actual] | 45 | 0.0006 | 0.0011 | 0.0017 | 0.0022 | 0.0027 | 0.0032 | 0.0037 | 0.0042 | 0.0047 | 0.0051 |
| Difference |  | 0.0020 | 0.0042 | 0.0062 | 0.0082 | 0.0103 | 0.0123 | 0.0143 | 0.0163 | 0.0182 | 0.0203 |
| Break even condition |  | 0.20% | 0.21% | 0.21% | 0.20% | 0.21% | 0.20% | 0.20% | 0.20% | 0.20% | 0.20% |

## Table VI: Projected Defined Benefit Plans Accruals for Plans in Absence of Freeze (plan level)

This table reports the estimated benefit accruals for plans that have been frozen relative to the several control groups of plans that have not been frozen. In Panel A we report the estimated accruals for freeze relative to non-freeze plans while in Panel B we report freeze and non-freeze plans with a cash balance feature. The estimation is fully described in the text. For freezes, the table shows the estimated accrual based on the age-service table for the year preceding the freeze. $dABO$ is the estimated benefit accrual for regular plans. $Non\text{-}freezes$ refer to the group of plans that have not been frozen during the sample period. $Ind\ Controls$ constrains the non-freezes group based on the 2-digit SIC code and year. $PS\ Match1$ selects a matched non-freezes group based on propensity scores calculated based on 2-digit SIC, ABO and year. $PS\ Match2$ selects a matched non-freezes group based on propensity scores calculated based on 2-digit SIC, ABO, year, and the funding ratio. $PS\ Match3$ selects a matched non-freezes group based on propensity scores calculated based on 2-digit SIC, ABO, year, and the funding ratio. ***, **, * indicates the statistical significance of 0.01, 0.05 and 0.1 of the difference between the estimated benefit accruals of freezes relative to the control group.

Panel A: dABO/Total assets, frozen plans versus non-frozen plan.

|  | N | Sig.(diff) | Year +1 | Year +2 | Year +3 | Year +4 | Year +5 | Year +6 | Year +7 | Year +8 | Year +9 | Year +10 |
|---|---|---|---|---|---|---|---|---|---|---|---|---|
| Freezes | 116 |  | 0.0041 | 0.0081 | 0.0119 | 0.0153 | 0.0185 | 0.0228 | 0.0258 | 0.0286 | 0.0312 | 0.0335 |
| Non-freezes | 4,896 | *** | 0.0026 | 0.0052 | 0.0077 | 0.0101 | 0.0124 | 0.0154 | 0.0177 | 0.0199 | 0.0220 | 0.0239 |
| Ind Controls | 1,634 | *** | 0.0026 | 0.0051 | 0.0077 | 0.0101 | 0.0125 | 0.0155 | 0.0179 | 0.0202 | 0.0224 | 0.0245 |
| PS Match1 | 116 | *** | 0.0022 | 0.0044 | 0.0066 | 0.0087 | 0.0108 | 0.0134 | 0.0155 | 0.0175 | 0.0195 | 0.0213 |
| PS Match2 | 116 | *** | 0.0023 | 0.0046 | 0.0069 | 0.0091 | 0.0112 | 0.0139 | 0.0161 | 0.0183 | 0.0203 | 0.0221 |
| PS Match3 | 116 | *** | 0.0022 | 0.0044 | 0.0065 | 0.0086 | 0.0106 | 0.0131 | 0.0151 | 0.0170 | 0.0189 | 0.0206 |

Panel B: dCB/Total assets, frozen plans versus non-frozen plans (defined benefit plans with a cash balance feature)

|  | N | Sig.(diff) | Year +1 | Year +2 | Year +3 | Year +4 | Year +5 | Year +6 | Year +7 | Year +8 | Year +9 | Year +10 |
|---|---|---|---|---|---|---|---|---|---|---|---|---|
| Freezes | 49 |  | 0.0026 | 0.0051 | 0.0076 | 0.0102 | 0.0126 | 0.0151 | 0.0175 | 0.0199 | 0.0223 | 0.0247 |
| Non-freezes | 1,641 | * | 0.0018 | 0.0037 | 0.0055 | 0.0073 | 0.0091 | 0.0109 | 0.0126 | 0.0143 | 0.0160 | 0.0177 |
| Ind Controls | 338 | ** | 0.0015 | 0.0029 | 0.0044 | 0.0058 | 0.0072 | 0.0086 | 0.0099 | 0.0113 | 0.0126 | 0.0140 |
| PS Match1 | 49 | * | 0.0018 | 0.0037 | 0.0056 | 0.0075 | 0.0093 | 0.0111 | 0.0129 | 0.0146 | 0.0164 | 0.0181 |
| PS Match2 | 49 | * | 0.0019 | 0.0038 | 0.0058 | 0.0077 | 0.0095 | 0.0114 | 0.0132 | 0.0150 | 0.0168 | 0.0186 |
| PS Match3 | 49 | * | 0.0019 | 0.0039 | 0.0059 | 0.0078 | 0.0097 | 0.0115 | 0.0134 | 0.0152 | 0.0169 | 0.0187 |

## Table VII: Decomposition of Accrual Differences Between Freeze and Non-Freeze Firms

This table decomposes the differences between freeze firms and propensity-score matched control plans into benefit-related parameters, demographic factors, and the size of the labor force relative to firm assets. In each panel, the starting point is the counterfactual prospective DB accruals for freeze plans. The characteristics of each plan are then replaced with those of the propensity score matched controls sequentially and cumulatively, and the prospective DB accruals are re-calculated.

|  | dABO/TA (Year +1) | dABO/TA (Year +5) | dABO/TA (Year +10) |
|---|---|---|---|
| Freezes | 0.0041 | 0.0185 | 0.0335 |
| *Sequential Changes in Characteristics to PS Match1* | | | |
| Plan level scaling | | | |
|   Sponsor Assets | 0.0057 | 0.0275 | 0.0537 |
|   Total Participants | 0.0031 | 0.0151 | 0.0312 |
| Plan age service distribution | | | |
|   Cell participants | 0.0026 | 0.0133 | 0.0282 |
|   Cell salaries | 0.0027 | 0.0131 | 0.0261 |
| Plan level assumptions | | | |
|   g (salary growth) | 0.0026 | 0.0125 | 0.0247 |
|   i (discount rate) | 0.0025 | 0.0123 | 0.0241 |
|   k (accrual factor) | 0.0022 | 0.0108 | 0.0213 |
| *Sequential Changes in Characteristics to PS Match2* | | | |
| Plan level scaling | | | |
|   Sponsor Assets | 0.0036 | 0.0174 | 0.0331 |
|   Total Participants | 0.0033 | 0.0157 | 0.0302 |
| Plan age service distribution | | | |
|   Cell participants | 0.0027 | 0.0136 | 0.027 |
|   Cell salaries | 0.0028 | 0.0137 | 0.0276 |
| Plan level assumptions | | | |
|   g (salary growth) | 0.0028 | 0.0137 | 0.0286 |
|   i (discount rate) | 0.0028 | 0.0143 | 0.0305 |
|   k (accrual factor) | 0.0023 | 0.0112 | 0.0221 |
| *Sequential Changes in Characteristics to PS Match3* | | | |
| Plan level scaling | | | |
|   Sponsor Assets | 0.0047 | 0.0215 | 0.041 |
|   Total Participants | 0.003 | 0.0143 | 0.0281 |
| Plan age service distribution | | | |
|   Cell participants | 0.0026 | 0.013 | 0.0259 |
|   Cell salaries | 0.0028 | 0.0137 | 0.0272 |
| Plan level assumptions | | | |
|   g (salary growth) | 0.0028 | 0.0135 | 0.027 |
|   i (discount rate) | 0.0028 | 0.0135 | 0.0271 |
|   k (accrual factor) | 0.0022 | 0.0106 | 0.0206 |

## Table VIII: Probability of Plan Freeze as a Function of Defined Benefit Accruals

This table shows the marginal effects from the probit estimation of the probability of a plan freeze. The dependent variable is 1 if the plan is frozen next year and zero otherwise. Plan-year observations after the plan has been frozen are excluded. *dABO/TA* is the estimated benefit accrual for regular plans, normalized by the total assets (*TA*) of the sponsor. *ABO* is the Accumulated Benefit Obligation and *Active Participants* (%) is the ratio between the number of active participants and the number of total participants, as reported in Form 5500. *Funding* (%) is defined as plan assets (*PA*) minus plan liabilities (or *ABO*) divided by plan liabilities. Both plan assets and plan liabilities are collected from Form 5500. *Unionized* is a categorical variable equal to 1 if the plan is represented by a union, and zero otherwise. *EBITDA/Sales* refers to earnings before interest, taxes and depreciation and amortization expenses, normalized by total sales. *Interest coverage* is the ratio between EBIT and the interest payments on debt. Standard errors clustered at the sponsored level are reported in parenthesis. * denotes significance at the 10% level, ** at the 5% level, at the 1% level.

| VARIABLES | (1) ME | (2) ME | (3) ME | (4) ME | (5) ME | (6) ME | (7) ME | (8) ME | (9) ME |
|---|---|---|---|---|---|---|---|---|---|
| dABO/TA | 2.060*** | 1.676*** | 1.431*** | 1.428*** | 1.797*** | 1.428*** | 1.563*** | 1.565*** | 1.147*** |
|  | (0.393) | (0.406) | (0.365) | (0.358) | (0.352) | (0.358) | (0.341) | (0.397) | (0.316) |
| ABO (log) | -0.006*** |  |  |  | -0.006*** |  | -0.005*** | -0.005*** | -0.004*** |
|  | (0.001) |  |  |  | (0.001) |  | (0.001) | (0.001) | (0.001) |
| ACTIVE PARTICIPANTS (%) |  | 0.022** |  | 0.019* |  | 0.019* |  |  |  |
|  |  | (0.011) |  | (0.010) |  | (0.010) |  |  |  |
| PLAN FUNDING |  |  | -0.042*** | -0.042*** | -0.036*** | -0.042*** | -0.037*** |  | -0.033*** |
|  |  |  | (0.011) | (0.011) | (0.010) | (0.011) | (0.010) |  | (0.010) |
| UNIONIZED |  |  |  |  |  |  | -0.014*** | -0.015*** | -0.014*** |
|  |  |  |  |  |  |  | (0.003) | (0.003) | (0.003) |
| EBITDA/ SALES |  |  |  |  |  |  |  | -0.009* | -0.003 |
|  |  |  |  |  |  |  |  | (0.005) | (0.004) |
| INTEREST COVERAGE |  |  |  |  |  |  |  |  | -0.000*** |
|  |  |  |  |  |  |  |  |  | (0.000) |
| Cluster SE (firm level) | YES | YES | YES | YES | YES | YES | YES | YES | YES |
| Observations | 5,123 | 5,165 | 5,123 | 5,123 | 5,123 | 5,123 | 5,123 | 5,051 | 4,710 |
| pseudo-r2 | 0.0343 | 0.0166 | 0.0312 | 0.0354 | 0.0515 | 0.0354 | 0.0655 | 0.0444 | 0.0754 |

## Table IX: *Ex Post* Salary growth

The table presents the actual salary growth before and after the freeze for freeze plans and their controls. *'Previous years'* refer to all years before the freeze and *'Year +1'* refers to the first year after the freeze was implemented. *Ind Controls* constrains the non-freezes group based on the 2-digit SIC code and year. *PS Match1* selects a matched non-freezes group based on propensity scores calculated based on 2-digit SIC, ABO and year. *PS Match3* selects a matched non-freezes group based on propensity scores calculated based on 2-digit SIC, ABO, year, and the funding ratio.

|  | N | Previous Years (MEAN) | Previous Years (MEDIAN) | Year +1 (MEAN) | Year +1 (MEDIAN) |
|---|---|---|---|---|---|
| Freezes | 72 | 4.35% | 4.40% | 2.56% | 3.14% |
| Industry controls | 1,150 | 4.41% | 4.41% | 4.86% | 3.78% |
| Freezes | 72 | 4.35% | 4.40% | 2.56% | 3.14% |
| PS Match1 | 72 | 4.44% | 4.53% | 5.72% | 4.91% |
| Freezes | 72 | 4.35% | 4.40% | 2.56% | 3.14% |
| PS Match3 | 72 | 4.07% | 4.26% | 5.31% | 3.90% |

## Figure 1: Estimated benefit factor

This figure shows the estimated benefit factor at the plan level, for all plans (freeze and non-freeze). The benefit factor is estimated based on past plan service cost (from Form 5500) and the age-service tables distributions of participants and salaries.

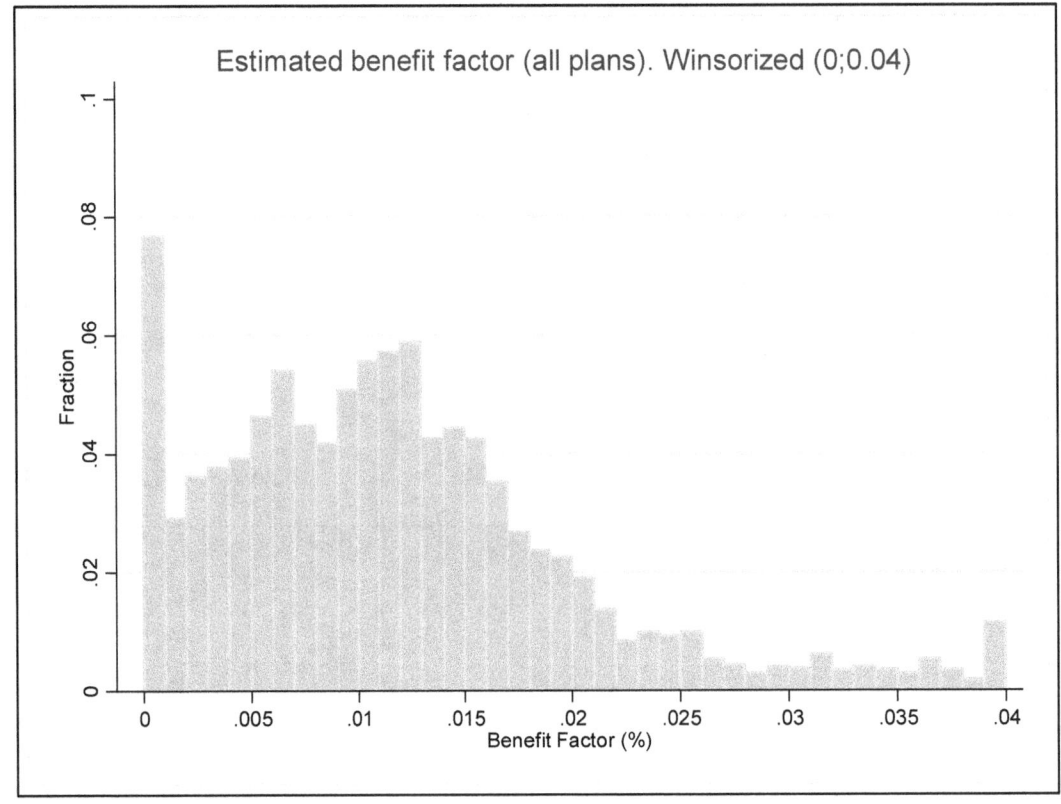

# Figure 2: Estimated Cost savings as a share of payroll by age groups

The figure shows the estimated cost savings projected 10 years into the future for three age groups: (a) 20-34 years old; (b) 35-49 years old; (c) 50-65 years old. The cost savings are calculated as the difference between the counterfactual accrual benefits and the actual change in 401(k) contribution, relative to the payroll and total sponsor assets.

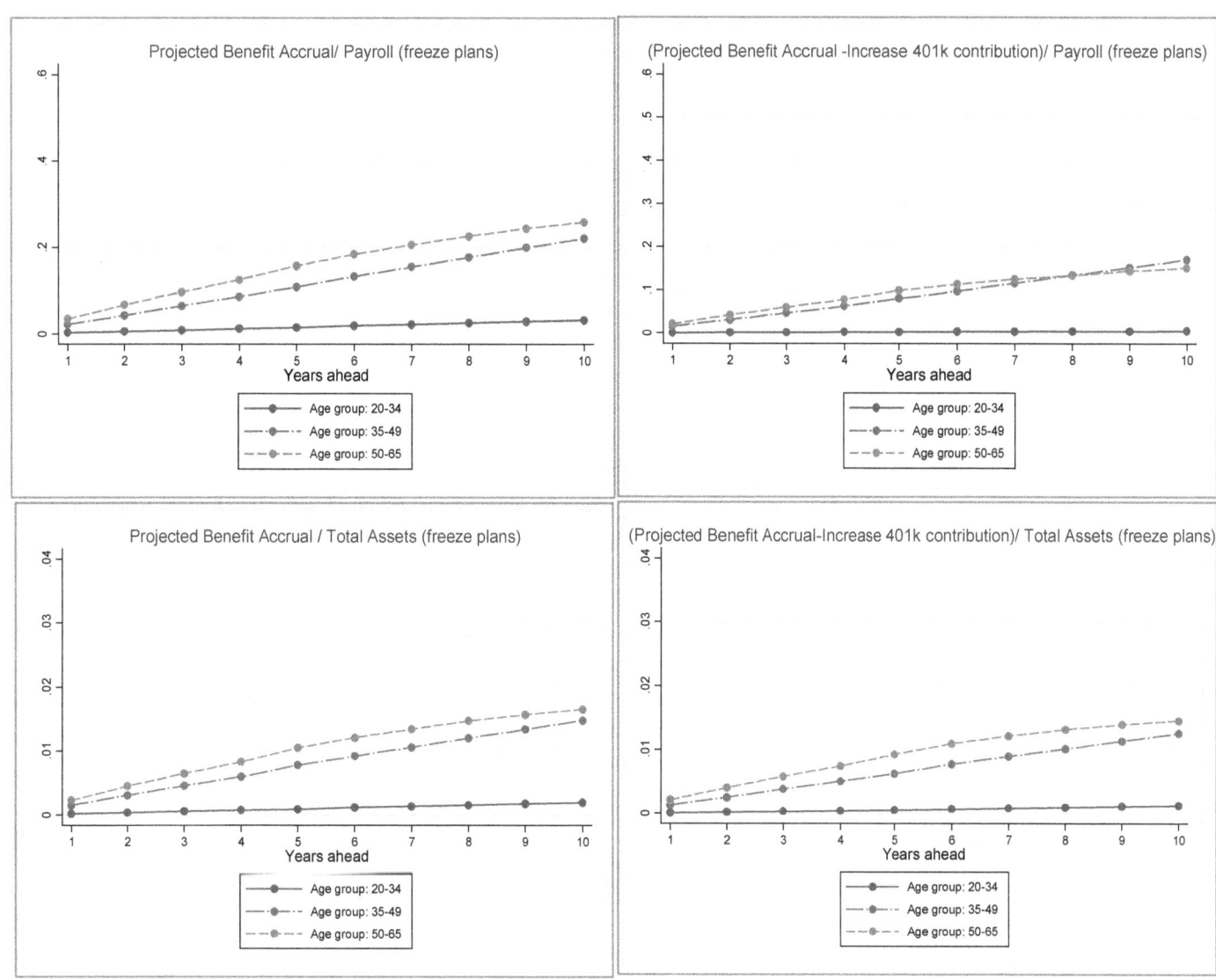

# Figure 3: Projected Benefit Accruals for Freezes and Controls

The table shows projected benefit accruals as a percentage of the payroll and of total sponsor assets (*TA*) for traditional Defined Benefit plans (Panel A) and Cash Balance plans (Panel B). Each graph includes estimates for three different groups: freezes, non-freezes, propensity control plans.

*Panel A: Benefit accruals for regular Defined Benefit plans*

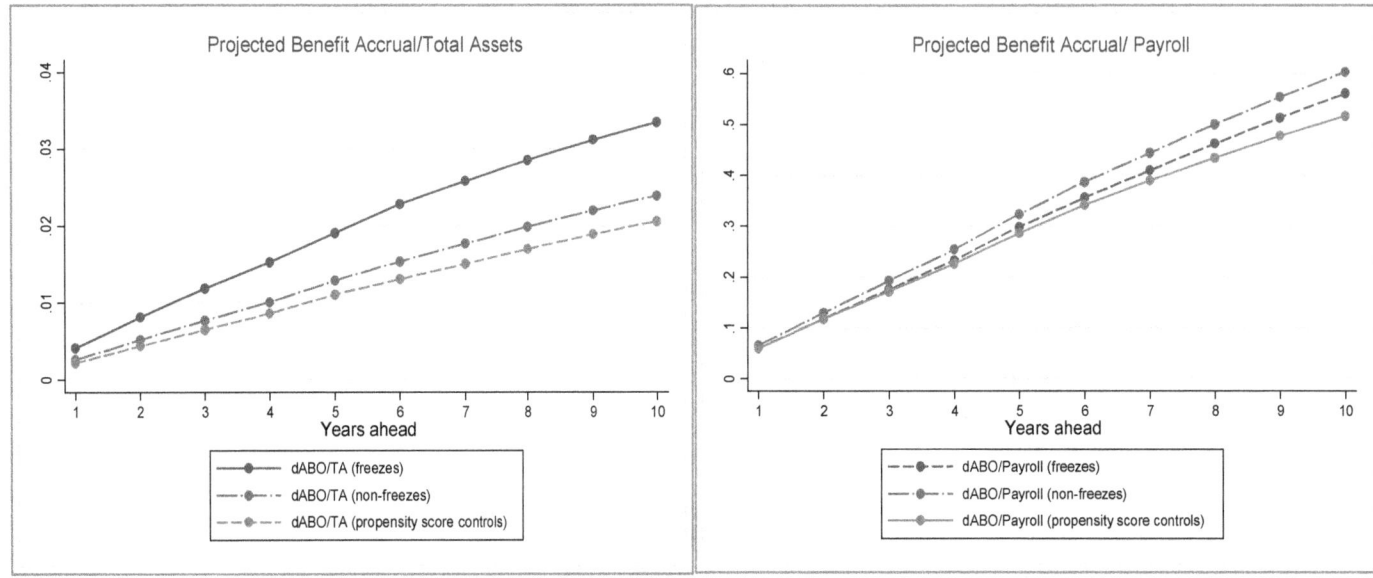

*Panel B: Benefit accruals for defined benefit plans with a Cash Balance feature*

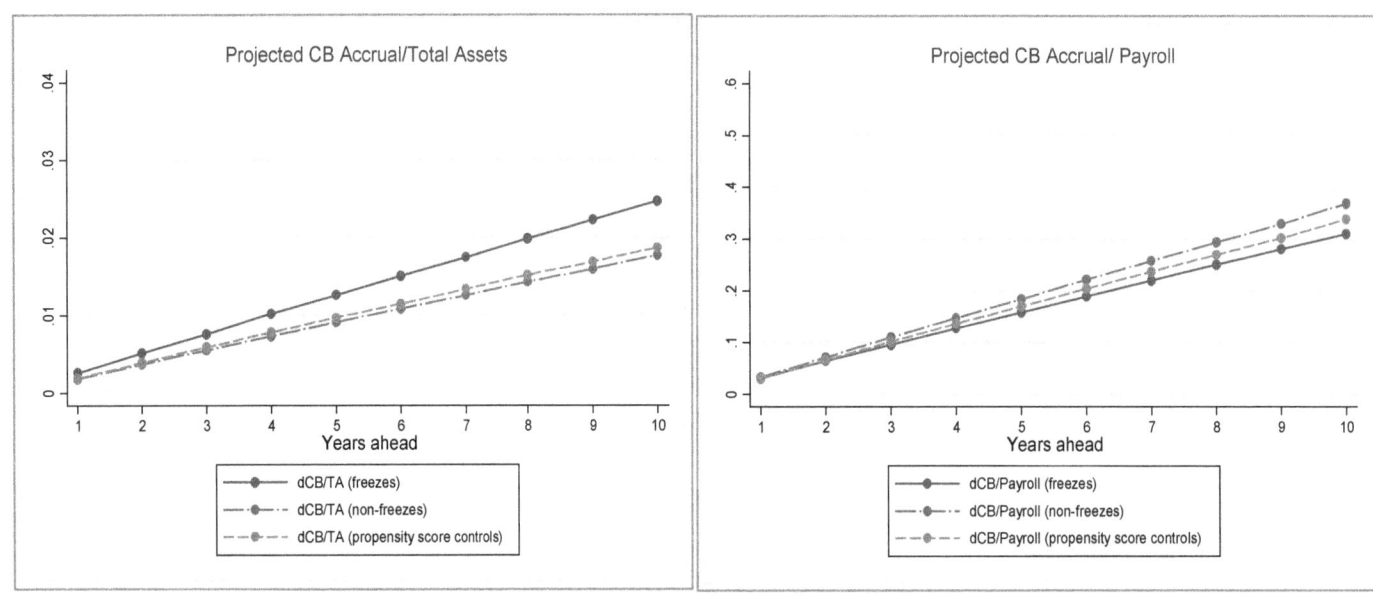

# Figure 4: Age-Service Distributions

The figure shows the age distribution (Panel A) and the service distribution (Panel B) for traditional pension plan freezes (left panel) and cash balance plan freezes (right panel). We include all plan years preceding the freeze.

*Panel A: Age distribution*

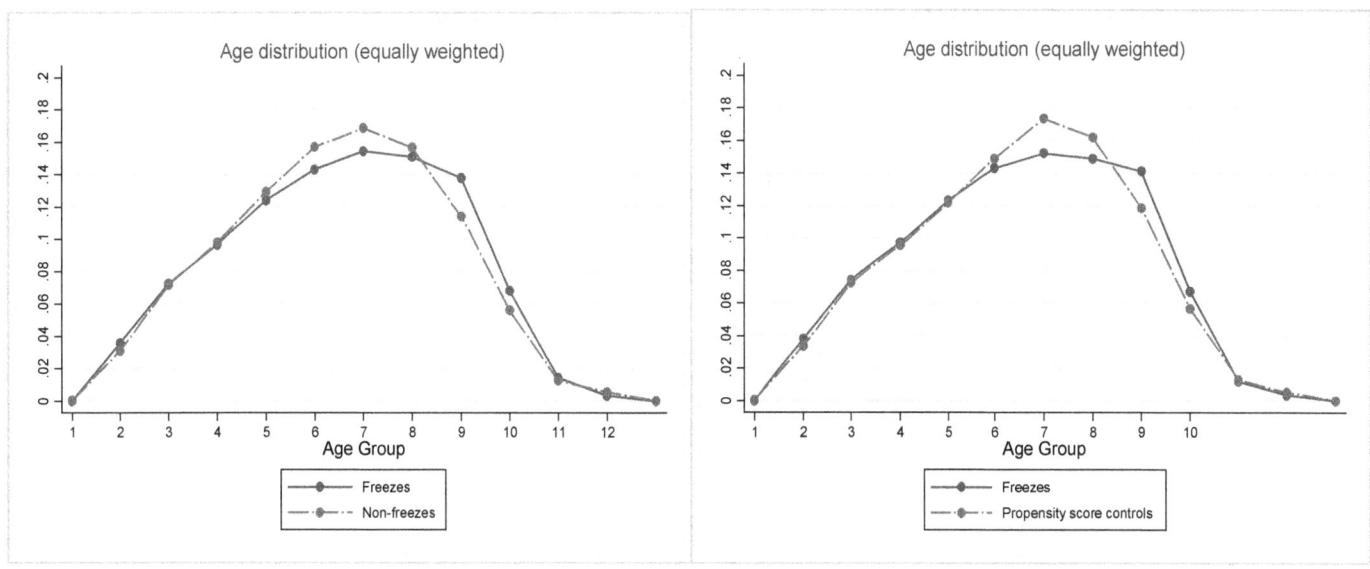

*Panel B: Service distribution*

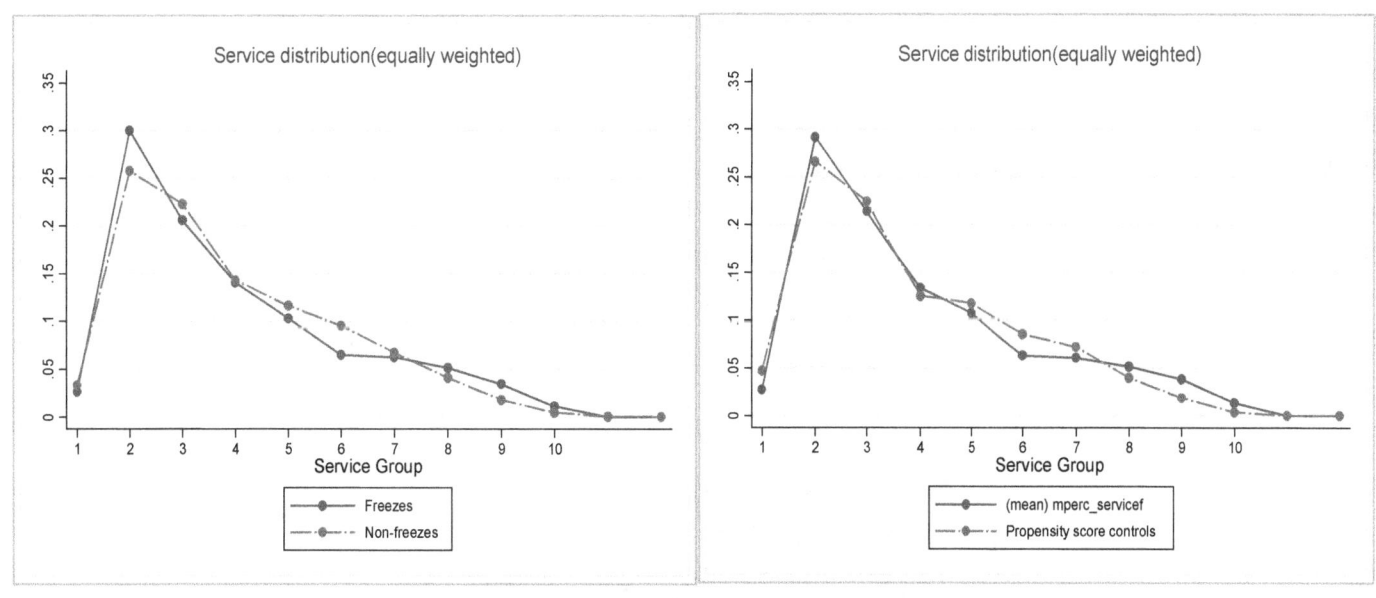

*Notes:*

| Age Group | 1 | 2 | 3 | 4 | 5 | 6 | 7 | 8 | 9 | 10 | 11 | 12 | 13 |
|---|---|---|---|---|---|---|---|---|---|---|---|---|---|
| Age | <20 | 20-24 | 25-29 | 30-34 | 35-39 | 40-44 | 45-49 | 50-54 | 55-59 | 60-64 | 65-69 | 70-74 | 75< |

| Service Group | 1 | 2 | 3 | 4 | 5 | 6 | 7 | 8 | 9 | 10 | 11 | 12 |
|---|---|---|---|---|---|---|---|---|---|---|---|---|
| Service | <1 | 1 4 | 5-9 | 10-14 | 15-19 | 20-24 | 25-29 | 30-34 | 35-39 | 40 | 45 | 50 |

## Figure 5: Age Service Distributions (alternative)

The figure shows the age-service distribution for freeze (Panel A) and non-freeze plans (Panel B). Panel C shows the plot of the difference between the age-service distribution of freeze and non-freeze plans. We include all plan years preceding the freeze.

*Panel A: Age Service Distribution (Freezes)*

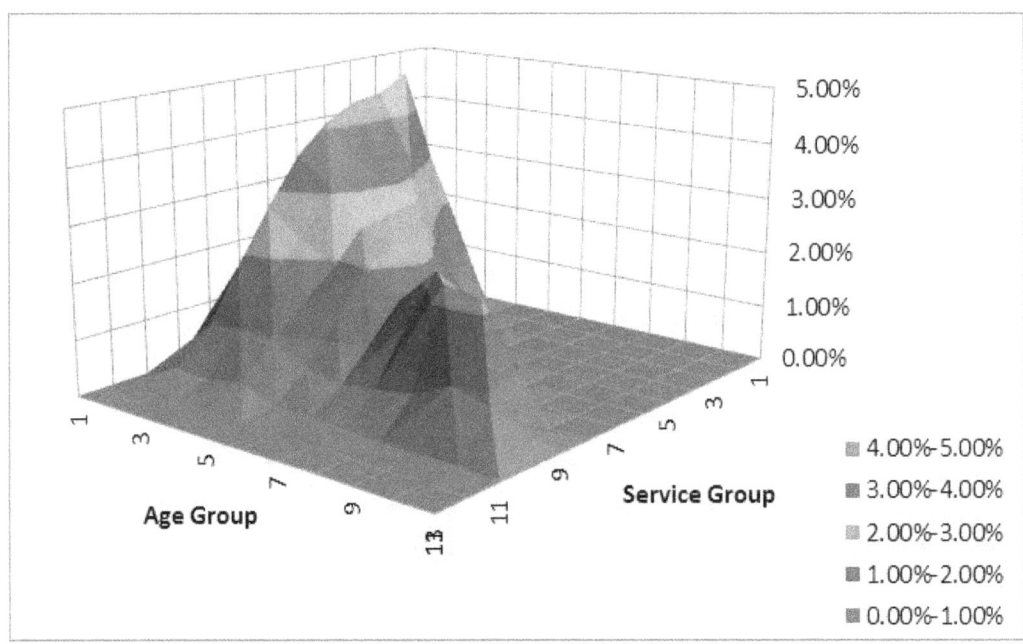

*Panel B: Age Service Distribution (Non Freezes)*

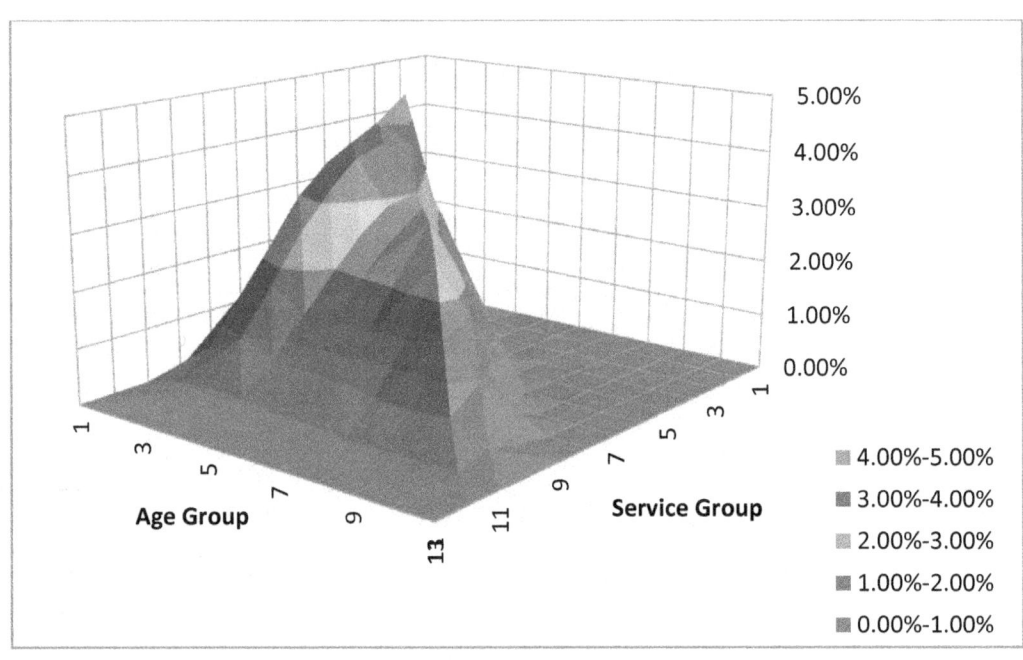

*Panel C: Difference Age Service Distributions (Freezes- Non Freezes)*

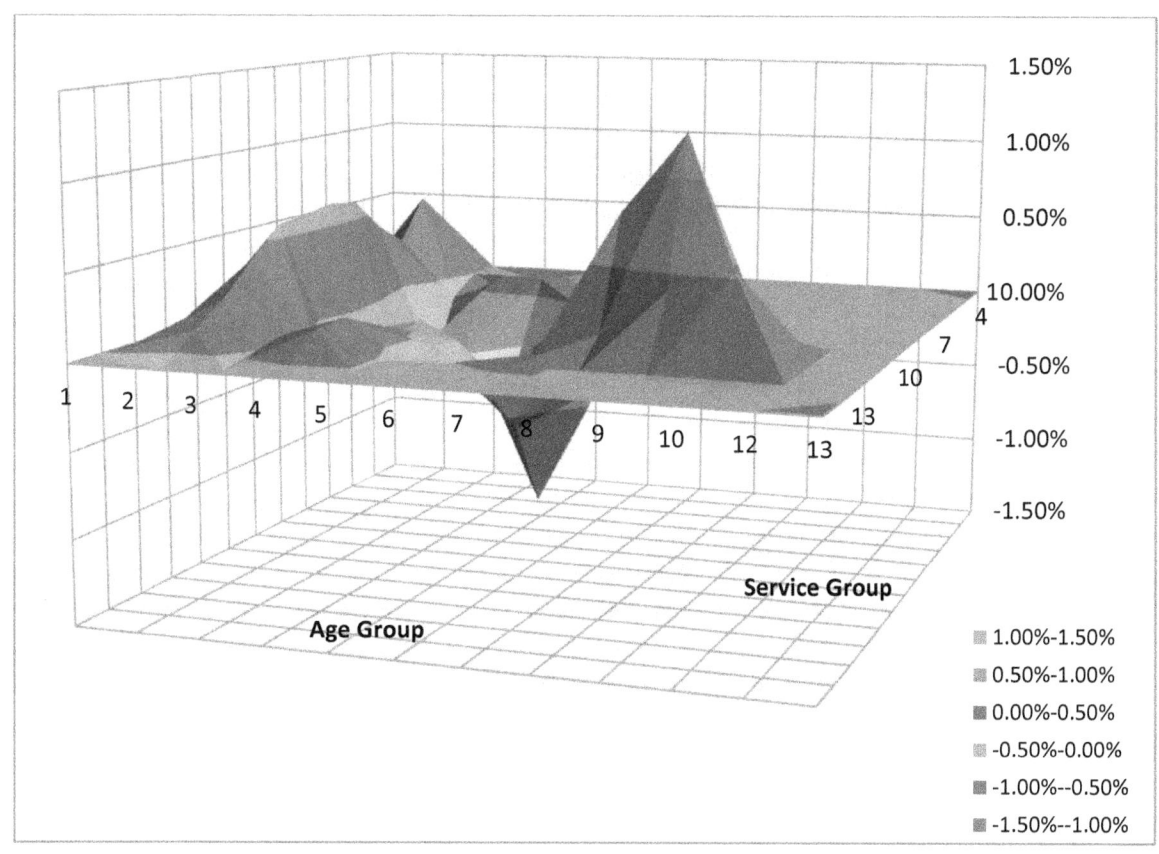

## Figure 6: Benefit Accruals by Age Groups for Freeze versus Control Plans

The figure shows the differences in projected benefit accruals for three different age groups: (a) 20-34 years old; (b) 35-49 years old; (c) 50-65 years old. The top graph shows benefit accruals for freeze plans relative to the control group, normalized by payroll. The bottom graph shows benefit accruals relative to the control group, normalized by the total sponsor assets (TA).

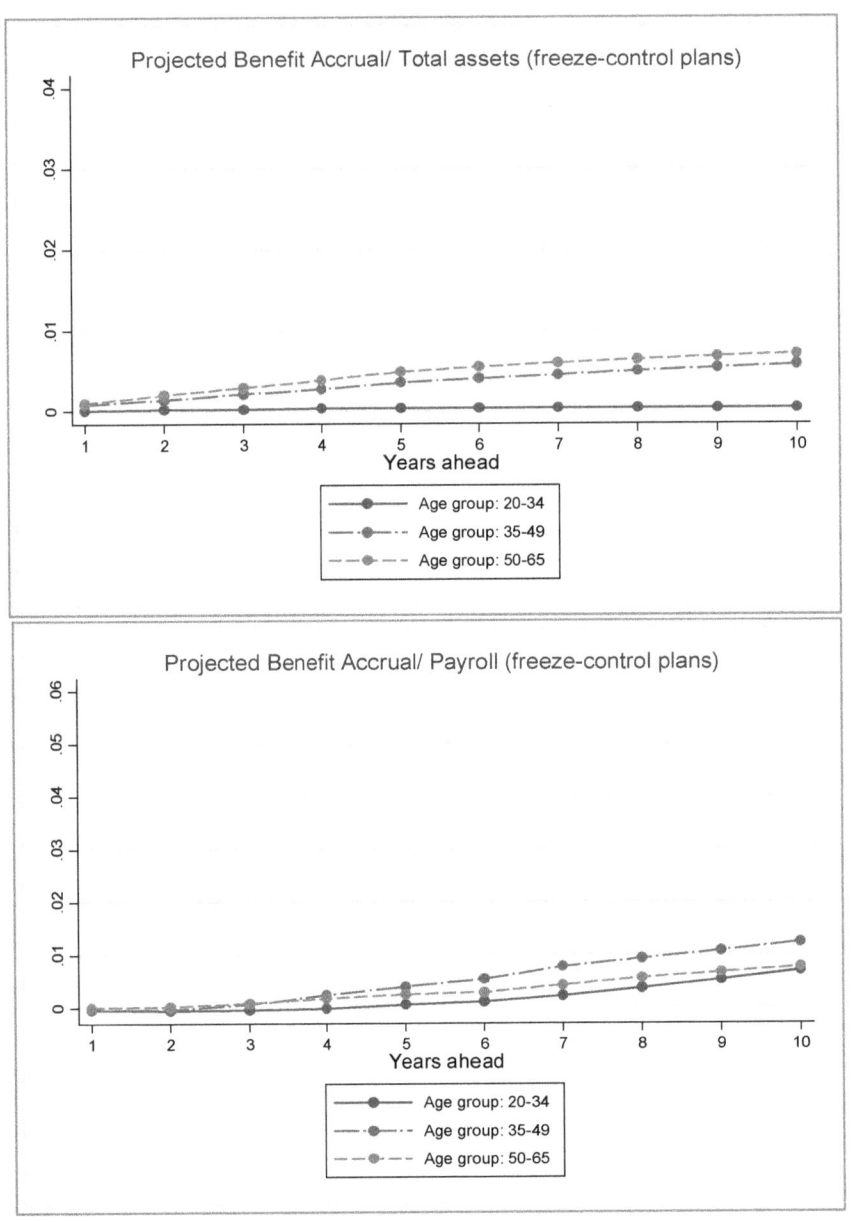

# Appendix: Example of Age-Service Matrix

This is an example of an age-service (and compensation) matrix, collected from the paper attachments to Form 5500.

| Attained Age | Years of Service | | | | | | | | | |
|---|---|---|---|---|---|---|---|---|---|---|
| | <1 | 1-4 | 5-9 | 10-14 | 15-19 | 20-24 | 25-29 | 30-34 | 35-39 | 40+ |
| <25 | 157 $37,272 | 297 $47,783 | 38 $46,381 | | | | | | | |
| 25-29 | 290 $45,609 | 1,877 $62,874 | 1,113 $64,188 | 28 $64,280 | | | | | | |
| 30-34 | 268 $48,594 | 2,037 $70,739 | 2,704 $71,797 | 678 $73,889 | 69 $70,838 | | | | | |
| 35-39 | 221 $49,442 | 1,367 $74,445 | 2,094 $75,538 | 1,437 $82,468 | 1,369 $83,476 | 70 $77,843 | | | | |
| 40-44 | 205 $53,620 | 1,047 $75,557 | 1,624 $77,173 | 1,049 $85,723 | 2,007 $90,267 | 2,373 $85,715 | 355 $78,478 | | | |
| 45-49 | 145 $49,954 | 638 $71,965 | 1,092 $75,501 | 690 $83,525 | 1,289 $91,437 | 3,410 $90,855 | 1,999 $87,143 | 406 $86,384 | | |
| 50-54 | 103 $51,393 | 428 $72,208 | 651 $73,844 | 432 $80,177 | 806 $87,100 | 1,060 $89,129 | 1,224 $91,712 | 1,696 $93,062 | 114 $88,210 | |
| 55-59 | 45 $51,026 | 248 $71,141 | 351 $77,044 | 239 $75,080 | 286 $82,843 | 271 $87,265 | 281 $91,771 | 564 $93,768 | 312 $91,462 | 21 $93,106 |
| 60-64 | 13 | 76 $66,371 | 120 $73,213 | 66 $68,061 | 50 $77,637 | 54 $70,217 | 52 $66,673 | 73 $87,677 | 96 $86,666 | 36 $86,447 |
| 65-69 | 3 | 12 | 15 | 5 | 4 | 3 | 3 | 7 | 5 | 14 |
| 70+ | | 1 | 1 | 6 | | 1 | | 2 | 1 | 2 |

Plan Name: Xerox Corporation Retirement Income Guarantee Plan  
EIN: 16-0468020  
PN: 333